THE HOME HAS A HEART

BOOKS BY THYRA FERRÉ BJORN

Papa's Wife

Papa's Daughter

Mama's Way

A Trilogy, *containing*
Papa's Wife, Papa's Daughter
and Mama's Way

Dear Papa

Once Upon a Christmas Time

This Is My Life

The Home Has a Heart

The Home
Has a Heart

THYRA FERRÉ BJORN

HOLT, RINEHART AND WINSTON
New York   Chicago   San Francisco

Published simultaneously in Canada by
Holt, Rinehart and Winston of Canada, Limited

Library of Congress Catalog Card Number: 68-11831

Published, September, 1968
Second Printing, November, 1968

Designer: Ernst Reichl
SBN: 03–068060–3
Printed in the United States of America

To
Deborah Lou,
my beloved granddaughter,
this book is lovingly dedicated

To my regular readers:

I am happy to share with you much of my own heart in this book. *The Home Has a Heart* is different from my other books. In it are recipes many people have asked for. So much of the cooking I learned from my own mother, known to many of you as Mama. Much of it is from my own kitchen—foods I have toyed with, improving the flavor and making them more exciting to serve. Some recipes were given to me by friends and I am very grateful to each one of you who, through the years, has helped me prepare the best for my family at mealtime. The Norwood Baptist Church Women's Club let me pick from their cookbook that gorgeous frozen fruit salad which was a favor at their banquet when I spoke. I know you will all be grateful to them. Otherwise, the recipes are not from cookbooks; they are strictly personal home cooking.

It has been fun writing about the home and its functions —a mixture of so many unique ingredients and patterns. Many of them you, too, are aware of in your own homes, but let these serve as a reminder of the importance of a happy home life.

You who are cooks with many years of experience, please bear with me if I emphasize what you know so well. Remember that many of my readers are young and inexperienced homemakers, and I have wanted to help new brides building in a new home. The Gold Nuggets are far from being unique, but they have been nuggets of gold for me. Some are old and some are new; some are for the hands, some for the mind, some for the soul. Use them as you need them.

As always, I have woven into the woof of my writing the importance of the spiritual, of worship and prayer, of love and integrity. This is my goal in all my books—to help lift the world a little higher, to make love shine a little brighter, to draw the heart a little closer to God.

Blessings on all of you who read my book.

My very best wishes always,

Thyra Ferré Bjorn

Longmeadow, Massachusetts
September 12, 1967

To my new readers:

The strange story of Papa and Mama, told in my first book, *Papa's Wife,* has been the foundation of all my books. Papa was a bachelor who never intended to be a husband and father. Mama, twenty-two years younger than he, had made up her mind to marry him, and nothing in heaven nor earth could stop her. He was a minister in a small church in Swedish Lapland when she entered his household as his maid. After five years, having failed to catch him, she left his parsonage and emigrated to America where she became a cook for a wealthy New York family. After a year, Papa took a vacation trip to New York and they met quite by accident in Central Park. Mama proposed to Papa, who finally gave in, and they were married. After a stormy first year, Mama presented Papa with a redheaded baby much to Papa's embarrassment, for next to sin he disliked red hair. Mama blamed it on the fact that she had to look at the janitor's redheaded boys in the front pew at church every Sunday, and Papa took it up from there. The janitor moved his little boys to the back pew, and Mama found a picture of an angel for a model.

Poor Papa ended up with eight children in all. The family moved to America where the happy story continues.

This brief introduction gives you some information about the Franzons—of Lapland, Sweden, and Massachusetts, U.S.A. In this book, for the first time, you will read of the older family branches who fit in so well with this latest writing.

I hope reading this book will give you the same joy I felt when I created it.

My very best wishes to you all,

Thyra Ferré Bjorn

Longmeadow, Massachusetts
September 12, 1967

~1

Dear Heavenly Father, for the gift of a New
Year we thank Thee, and for the fact that the
unknown days ahead will be guided by Thy
strong hand. For this new book, too, I express
my gratitude, for the thoughts that are given
me to be expressed in sentence after sentence
and chapter after chapter, for words that sing
and pray and laugh and cry.

Life is so full of wonder and beauty! If we
begin each new day with Thy love in our
hearts, it will surely be a good year, Blessed
Lord. Amen.

"AND what will you write next?" asked a
friend, holding a copy of my most recent book.

The question caught me unaware and my answer came
before I had time to think it through.

"Who knows? I might write a cook book!"

"That would be great!" My friend laughed. "I'd like to
see you do a book like that. And I predict it would be

different—not just recipes, but stories along with them."

That kindled the idea, and I toyed with it for a while. Then suddenly I knew that that was the type of book I would write next.

I began it on a beautiful January morning. Within me was that excited, mysterious feeling that always seems to overtake me when I write the first sentence of a new book. It was strange, I thought, that I was sitting in my dining room. Although I had written in many corners of the house, I didn't remember having set up my typewriter in this room before. It must have been the view from the window that had drawn me there. Outside it was snowy and cold, but the garden looked beautiful clad in white with what seemed like hundreds of birds of all kinds eating lustily from the three feeders. Others seemed to be having a siesta in the tall pine tree.

How that pine has grown! It is almost as wide as it is tall.

A few years ago, when I was visiting friends in the mountains of Vermont, I tramped through the woods on a lovely spring afternoon, and pulled up two small trees —a pine and a spruce. They were only two feet tall when I had planted them in our backyard. And how many good laughs we as a family had had about those trees simply because I gave them names. The pine was called Clinton and the spruce, Florence, after my Vermont friends. Both trees thrived on all the attention they received and it was as if they started a race to see which one could grow the taller. Clinton was the leader, eventually exceeding the height of our ranch home, but Florence was not far behind.

My husband doesn't like too many trees near the house, though I would love to have a whole yard full of them.

Many times, as the pine began to take on height, Bob would threaten, "Someday when you're away, I'm going to chop down Clinton."

"You wouldn't dare!" I'd answer. "How could you do a thing like that to a tree named Clinton?"

But the pine tree still stands, and Bob hasn't mentioned cutting it down for a long time now. I think that is probably because he is such a bird lover and the birds love our pine. It has become a sanctuary for them, especially on winter days. It is a cozy shelter in a time of storm, much as a home is to a family.

It must have been that scene that drew me into the dining room, and what better place could there be to start a cook book than in a room which so often bulged with happy people gathered in good fellowship around our dining-room table? It was not just the food that had made the room; it was the atmosphere—the warmth, the times of fun and laughter and, yes, times of sorrow when the family had gathered and tears had flowed freely. This added up to a home that brought out that sweet closeness of hearts.

And that will be the theme of this book—not only food and how to prepare it, but the heart of the home, which must be a healthy heart beating strongly through the many years that a home stands.

Every home must have a heart, even our somewhat different space-age homes. Is that what is wrong with America? Can it be that the heart of the home has an illness? Like the physical heart, the heart of the home suffers casualties. When it has an attack and is not attended to in time, it stops beating and the home is dead. Love is gone and the home breaks into little pieces. The inhabitants are scattered and the dear place that once was is no more.

Much has been written about the divorce rate that seems to be increasing instead of decreasing. It affects not only the rich or the poor, but everyone, everywhere —people of every faith, of every race, of every color. It is an illness—a terrible illness when the home has heart disease.

Always when I write, I like to go back in time. I like to turn back the years as one would turn the pages in a book—one by one until I go as far back as I can remember. How long has this heart disease been going on? Almost every homemaker, in every generation, has had and still has a part in the building up or the breaking down of the home. And when what we have done is bad, we all suffer from it, because when the home suffers, the whole nation suffers.

A long time ago—so many years ago that I could almost write "once upon a time"—the pride of a woman's life was her home. Cooking to her was an art and even though there were few fancy ingredients readily available, she had a magic touch. By taking a pinch of this and a handful of that, using so many shakes and so many strokes, she would create in her mixing bowl a substance that, when baked in a wood stove without temperature control, would come out to perfection. But the biggest ingredient, always sprinkled liberally into all mixtures, was love. And the atmosphere that surrounded the cook was one of gratefulness—for being alive, being married, having a large family to cook for, a house to live in, and pots and pans and all the other household tools to work with. The home did not need to be furnished elaborately. It had other attributes—the aroma of bread baking in the oven, the smell of soup simmering on the stove, the scent of delicately spiced meats. These were the things that made the menfolk set their feet toward home when day was done and brought the children bouncing into the kitchen tired and happy from play.

That housewife did not need to use rouge on her cheeks. The roses painted there were done by Mother Nature and contained the glow of love and excitement.

Yes, that was a different life from the one in our push-button world of today; it had room for peace and gentleness and togetherness. Thankfulness was a virtue and those people possessed it; they knew how to appreciate life. Those women did not have the education of today's housewife, but they did possess wisdom and with that key they unlocked the wonders of each new day. And in spite of all they had to do, they seemed to have time left over just to sit and think and dream and be happy.

I want to take time in this book to relive those years. I'd like to take time to tell some stories and to try to see the good side of this age. We have so very, very much to make life easy for us. We live in a magic world and if we add happiness to it, our age will glow more brightly than any other on earth because there is still so much goodness, kindness, and joy left in our world. We must be grateful for all the new things which a few years ago no one ever dreamed would exist. So let us be thankful to God for everything—the old and the new.

In olden days each meal started with thankfulness. Families bowed their heads in grace and asked God to bless their labor, their food, their loved ones. It is a lovely picture, that table scene, and in my mind I can hear the words in unison from young and old alike:

> God is great and God is good.
> Lord, we thank Thee for this food.
> Thank you for another day.
> Bless it, Lord, we humbly pray.
> Amen.

But times were not always good and often folks were thankful even for very little.

Long, long before I came into this world, when my Papa was a little boy in Sweden in the early 1870's, there were years of famine. The cause of it I do not know, but there were lean years for many, especially the poor. Papa, who came from a poor family of fourteen children, often told us about those years. Many times he had to go out to beg for bread, which was very hard on him because he was a sensitive, shy child. His younger brother, Herman, was often sent out with him, and together they tramped the dusty roads toward the country and the farms. It seemed that the farm people always had bread to eat.

One summer day, the hottest Papa could ever remember, he and Herman had walked for miles and miles with nothing to show for their travels but ridicule and slammed doors. They had blisters on their feet and were very tired as they approached a large red and white farmhouse set back from the road in a cool garden with large trees.

"I'm afraid to knock on that door, Frans," said Herman as they walked hand in hand to the back door.

"We have to get some bread, Herman. The whole family is waiting at home for us. How can we go back without bringing anything?"

"It isn't our fault that no one will give us any food."

"Perhaps we'll have better luck here," whispered Frans, squeezing his brother's small hand.

There was a long pause after they knocked. Then finally they heard footsteps. The door swung open and a large friendly woman smiled at them.

"Well, well," she said, "what have we here? Some beggar children, if I guess right."

Frans nodded. "Would you kindly give us some bread?" he asked shyly.

"Yes," she said, "I'll give you a loaf." She hurried into her kitchen and soon reappeared with a large round loaf of bread.

"Here, take this," she said kindly.

Both boys bowed and thanked her. A whole loaf! That had never happened before. They could hardly believe their good fortune.

The woman patted Herman's head. "Poor little boy," she said. "You look so warm. You must be thirsty too."

"Yes, I'm very thirsty," whispered Herman hopefully.

"You poor child. I'll fetch you a mug of milk."

She went back to the kitchen and soon returned with a large mug filled to the brim with milk.

Herman took it gratefully, but when he tasted it, his face turned pale. The milk had turned; it was going sour. And turned milk was something Herman's stomach wouldn't take. He felt sick, but he didn't dare to complain. The woman might become angry and take back her loaf of bread. He had to drink the milk. So that he wouldn't taste it for too long, he swallowed it in one big gulp.

As the woman watched him, tears came to her eyes.

"I've never seen such a thirsty little fellow," she said. "I'll refill your mug."

Though Herman felt ill, there was nothing to do but drink it. They couldn't hurt the kind woman's feelings. Frans looked on anxiously, unable to help, as Herman made sure that this time he drank the milk very slowly. Then they both thanked the woman again and started down the dusty road. Herman just made it to the bend in the road where he was a very sick little boy.

When they reached home and told their story, their parents said the boys had done the right thing. They were proud of their sons and that seemed to make up for everything.

What a treat it was that night, Papa told us, to sit around the table with that big family. Their one cow was still giving milk, and the bread was fresh. There was enough so that each of them had one big slice, except the baby who was too young to eat bread. And even in their poverty there was a togetherness; no matter how little they had, home was still the dearest place on earth.

It is strange how that story stuck in my mind as a child. I lived it over and over. I could see the two poor little boys on that dusty road—tired, hungry, and longing for home. How glad I was that I did not need to beg, that we always had plenty of food even if we were a large family, and I thanked God for home and food and family. It was hard to picture my handsome, learned, dignified

Papa as that poor little boy. Yet, in spite of the poverty that surrounded him as a child, he worked his way through school, graduating with honors from the theological seminary in Stockholm, which proves that nothing can stop a person from reaching his goal in life if he really sets out to get there. I knew that I, too, could become what I wanted to. Was that why Papa had told us that story—to teach us all those things? Most of all, I think, he wanted to teach his own children to be grateful.

Although I never met my *Farmor,* my father's mother, who died before I was born, I shall share with you some recipes she might have used in her home and which still are used in Sweden.

This menu is for a cold day, so let us picture a day in January. The wind is blowing the white snow into huge drifts outside the window. The cold outside makes the warmth and coziness of home dearer than ever.

Here is our menu for that day:

ENTREE

Cooked, smoked lean shoulder
Rot-mos   Tomato slices
Freshly baked rye bread with butter

DESSERT

Swedish fruit soup with whipped cream
Coffee   Milk

The rye bread has to be set the first thing in the morning so let us start with that recipe.

SWEDISH RYE BREAD

2½ cups milk
½ cup shortening
1 cup corn syrup (light)
½ cup dark molasses
½ teaspoon aniseed
½ teaspoon fennel seed
½ teaspoon caraway seed

1 level tablespoon salt
2 packages of yeast (dissolved in a little lukewarm water)
4 cups rye flour
5 cups white flour

Heat the milk and add shortening, syrup, molasses, and spices. Remove from the stove when the mixture is lukewarm and add yeast and salt. Place the two flours in a big bowl and mix them thoroughly. Add liquid and work with your hand until everything is mixed well and is pliable. Set this aside, covered with a towel, until it is double in size. Place dough on a baking board and knead. Divide the dough into three sections and place in long bread pans that have been well greased. (If a wide pan is used bread will not be done in the middle.) Sprinkle each loaf with a little flour and let stand until the dough is again double in size. Bake in a moderate oven (350°) about 40 minutes or until a toothpick inserted into the bread comes out clean. After removing the bread from the oven, brush with syrup-water made from 1 teaspoon corn syrup and and 1 tablespoon water.

If the bread is to be eaten warm, slice lightly with a sharp knife. Do not press hard.

ROT-MOS

1 yellow turnip cut in chunks
twice as much raw potato cut in chunks
one lean smoked shoulder
3 tablespoons margarine
Salt and pepper to taste

Place the smoked shoulder in a large kettle and boil until almost done. Add the turnip and boil for an additional 20 minutes. Add potatoes and boil another 10 minutes. When the vegetables are thoroughly done, remove kettle from heat and drain off the water. Remove the meat. Add margarine to the vegetables and mash until they are light and fluffy. Add salt and pepper to taste.

When ready to serve, arrange the slices of meat on a round platter and heap the turnip-potato mixture in the middle. Place a few thinly sliced tomatoes here and there, and decorate with a few sprigs of parsley.

SWEDISH FRUIT SOUP

       1 package of mixed dried fruit
      ½ cup raisins
      ½ cup sugar
       1 slice lemon
         a bit of a whole cinnamon stick
       1 pint grape juice
       1 glass jar of Queen Anne cherries (pitted)
       5 cups water
      1½ teaspoons potato starch dissolved in water

Place the dried fruit, raisins, sugar, lemon, and cinnamon in water and boil for 30 minutes. Remove from heat and add grape juice, pitted cherries, and juice. When the soup is cold, add the potato-starch mixture. Place over heat and bring to a slow boil. Boil soup for 1 minute. Remove from heat and pour into a bowl. Cool and serve with a heaping spoonful of whipped cream. (Serves eight)

On a chilly night when the family will arrive home cold and weary, see that the table has a bright cloth and add, perhaps, some fresh evergreens in a low container as a centerpiece. Don't ever think of husband and children as "just the family." Fuss a bit for them and you will be rewarded. Be sure the silver is straight and even at each place, and the napkins folded neatly. Make each meal the most important task you have ever undertaken. See that all the family members eat at the same time if possible. This is an important factor for a growing family, for nothing can take the place of togetherness. And when your children have grown up and look back to these memories, a glow will fill their hearts that will spill over into their own family life.

GOLD NUGGET:

To remove the pits from cherries use an old-fashioned buttonhook. Place the hook in the stem end of the cherries and pull the pits out carefully.

❧2

As the days of this month begin to pass into eternity, we thank Thee, God, for the joy of living each one—for laughter and fun and even for moments of pain and sorrow. We thank Thee for home and family, for good food, and for the hands which work so tirelessly to make our home a foretaste of Thy heaven. Amen.

EVEN though January is never a dull month, I am always glad to see it end. Much of the glow of Christmas spreads into the first part of January and much has to be done before the house gets back to normal, which makes the time speed by. No matter how beautiful the Christmas decorations have been, it feels good to take them down and pack them away neatly in their special boxes until next December. And all the gifts that have been on display for a while are also put away. Last, I think, are the Christmas cards. How many times I look at mine after the holidays have passed! But then

13

comes that day when I take one final long look and away they go into a bag for a mission which uses them in their work with children. I'm glad I can give them to such a place, for they are certainly far too beautiful to be destroyed.

But by the time February arrives, all of Christmas is gone and the little tasks belonging to the aftermath of the holidays have been taken care of. It almost seems that the New Year really begins in February because then everything does have a new look. It is such a dear, short month that I feel as if a loyal old friend has returned to visit me for a while.

True the days are still dark and snowstorms come and the weather is often extremely cold, but it is a time that gives us a chance to send our roots deeper into the home soil. Our fireplace burns almost every night and sometimes Bob and I play some soft music or a dear old Swedish hymn on the hi-fi, and a certain coziness settles down over the house. And I think, as I snuggle up on the rose-colored divan, that this really is home! And watching the wind blow outside the big picture window I know that it won't be long until spring, when the sun is warm on the earth and the days are longer and we bid farewell to Old Man Winter. At times like this I often think of the dear ones who are no longer a part of our earth life, and I know within my heart that age is creeping up on us and that we, too, may soon shed our earthly garments and go toward spring and light and a beautiful golden eternity in God's home for our souls. Then suddenly I think of my *Mormor* (my mother's mother).

My *Mormor* was different from any other person I have

ever known—the sweetest and dearest, and I loved her very much. She passed away on the first of March, 1917, so February was her last month on earth, and it is good to think of her as I write in this month. She was a tiny person, only a little over five feet tall, with the biggest, brightest blue eyes I have ever seen. On her silver hair she wore a lovely lace cap that gave her a certain dignity and grace. Her step was as light as if she had tiny wings on her feet. And *Mormor* always had time to spare for her grandchildren.

Since *Morfar* (my mother's father) was dead, *Mormor* lived alone in a tall white house by a lovely lake in the province of Närke in Sweden. It was very, very far from our parsonage, which was in the extreme northern part of the country, so we did not get to visit her very often. But some of the golden summer days that we spent with her when Mama took us on that long journey still linger in my memory.

Perhaps one of the reasons I feel so close to my *Mormor* is that she, too, was a writer, and I'm sure that my writing talent and vivid imagination come from her. But *Mormor*'s writing was never recognized. It was only after her death that the family discovered the boxes of manuscripts and poems that had flowed from her pen. But because the writing was so personal, revealing her innermost thoughts and dreams, they destroyed everything and it was lost and forgotten. But I couldn't forget. How very much I would have liked to have just one of those poems to read and re-read.

Now as I think of those days, I can remember standing at the kitchen window in *Mormor*'s home, looking down on the blue lake. My Mama had told me many stories about the lake from which in childhood she had learned many valuable lessons. There was a landing made of wooden planks jutting out into the water where a boat was tied. It was on that landing that Mama had learned her first hard lesson in obedience. We children were forbidden to walk out on the landing and the same rule had applied to my Mama long ago. Some people said that the lake was so deep that it had no bottom. Others said that once, back in the dark ages, there had been a cave where the lake now stood and that was why no one could ever measure its depth.

Mama had told me that as a child the landing had fascinated her. More than anything else she could think of, she had wanted to walk out on it. Then one day when her parents seemed to be very busy around the house, she took the chance. She had planned to stay only a minute or so, but time seemed to disappear as she lay flat on her stomach looking down into the deep blue-green water at the end of the landing. She was sure that a beautiful mermaid lived at the bottom. She wanted only a glimpse of her. Perhaps she could even talk her into coming ashore to play a game. Looking down into the water gave little Maria a strange feeling. It was as if a magnet drew her nearer and nearer and it seemed that a mysterious voiceless voice said, "Come, my child! Come down into the deep! It is cool and calm and beautiful! You will love the deep!"

Maria had all she could do to keep herself away from the water. Before she knew it, her hand had touched the water and then suddenly, without warning, she was drifting down into the deep, head first. She felt as if someone had a tight grip on her feet. She fought to free herself and get to the surface again. The water was dark and cold and she felt her lungs filling up. It was as if all her life just flickered away and she remembered no more. . . .

When Maria opened her eyes, she was in her own bed under lots of blankets, but she was as cold as ice and shivering from head to foot and her hair was very, very wet. So it hadn't been just a dream although she wished it had been. In the doorway stood her own Papa, his otherwise kindly face grim and his voice harsh as he said to her, "I hope you have learned your lesson!"

Maria stared at him as if she could not believe what she was thinking, and then she began to cry bitterly.

"It was you, Papa, who almost drowned me! You pushed me down under the water!"

"Yes, it was I. I hope you'll never forget how it felt to be down there under the water. I hope you've had enough of that lake."

Mama did not get a spanking, and she did understand the lesson her Papa had been trying to teach her even though it hurt her deeply to think that he had sneaked up on her, pushed her into the lake, and held her there until she had lost consciousness—all to teach her to obey.

Maria did keep away from the landing after that. No one could have made her set foot on it. But a few weeks later the lake provided her with another lesson.

It was a sunny fall afternoon when her Mama handed her a pail and asked her to go into the woods to the well to fetch some drinking water. It was a long, long walk to the well and the path wound through the deep woods, and my Mama just did not feel like walking all that way. Then an idea popped into her head.

How would anyone know whether she brought home well water or lake water? The lake water was cool and clear, too. Who would know the difference?

She knew she must not return too early or she would be found out. So she took her time. When she was out of the house, she flopped down in the wilted grass by the roadside. She lay on her back watching a beautiful bird on a tree limb. How would it feel to be a bird, she wondered, to have nothing to do but fly all day under the clear blue sky? Birds did not have to carry water, or do dishes, or darn socks.

Maria stayed in the grass a long while after the bird had flown away and when she thought enough time had passed, she walked down to the lake and stood on a stone and dipped the pail full. The water was very clear indeed and Maria was pleased as she walked home and into the kitchen, placed the pail on the water bench, and put the dipper in it. All was well until long after supper when it had been dark for hours and her Papa went to the pail and took a dipperful of water. It had barely touched his lips when it came down again furiously.

"Klara, you have mixed the water pails. This is lake water in the drinking pail."

"It can't be," said *Mormor.* "Maria fetched that water from the well this afternoon."

Poor Maria, she felt so frightened and remorseful and her heart was beating faster and faster. Why in the world had she done it?

"Maria," said her Papa, "where did you get this water?"

Maria hung her head. She stared at the floor.

"It is from the lake, Papa, because it is too far for a little girl like me to walk all the way to that well. The lake is so much closer and the water there was clear and cool, too."

Morfar shook his head. "You have another lesson to learn, my child, and I hope you'll learn it well, so I won't have to be so hard on you again."

Morfar emptied the water outside the kitchen door and then handed the pail and a lantern to little Maria.

"Here," he said, not unkindly, "take this and go to the well and fetch the water. And be sure you go all the way this time."

Maria cried and pleaded. "But, Papa, it is dark and it is a long way. I'm afraid and I might get lost in the woods."

"You should have thought of that when the sun was shining," said *Morfar*.

So Maria started out that night on her long walk to the well. She had never been more frightened. What a black night it was! And in her imagination there were trolls in the woods, terrible giants behind the mountains, and worst of all were the goblins who sometimes took little girls who were bad. Maria ran, stumbled, fell, and cried, and then started all over again; but she got to the well and brought home the water, and never again was she even tempted to get it from the lake. She had learned another lesson.

I cried when my Mama told me that story.

"Your Papa was mean!" I stormed angrily. "How could he have done that to you?"

But Mama only smiled.

"I've blessed him for it many times, my little one. He did what was best for me. You see, he knew that one day I would grow to be a mama myself and have little girls to bring up and he wanted me to teach them to do what was right."

"And you have, Mama," I confirmed. "You never let me get away with things."

Mama winked at me. "And when you bring up your girls, I want you to remember that whatever good you teach them when they are young will remain with them when they grow older. That is why it's so important to teach a child to do the right thing even if it seems trivial at the time."

"I'll try to remember that always," I said.

"Strictness," said Mama, "is love turned inside out, and you have to learn to be strict even with yourself. When a small inner voice tells you not to do a thing, listen to it. For if you don't listen, the next time the voice will be much softer, so that you can hardly hear it. And if you keep on ignoring it, someday it will not whisper at all."

I am glad that I had to learn obedience in my home, and I hope that my girls feel the same way about my strictness with them, because this helps make the home happy and healthy. And to keep the home happy, goodness must have its place.

Gratefulness was also instilled within us. There was a zinc mine near *Mormor*'s home and every Easter Eve the management of that mine treated the village people to refreshments. When we visited there at Easter, we all would walk with *Mormor* up the long hill to the top of the mine.

There, the small pail we carried was filled with a light ale, and *Mormor* was given a chunk of meat and a round loaf of bread. There was nothing more exciting to us children than that treat. I can see us now sitting around *Mormor*'s kitchen table preparing to eat. Yet before we could start, she would say, "First, let us thank God!"

Then she prayed a beautiful prayer which I remember so well. With her hand resting on the loaf of bread, she lifted her face toward heaven. She was radiantly beautiful and it seemed as if a ring of glory surrounded her:

> "We thank Thee Lord for this good gift.
> Our hearts are light; our heads we lift
> To praise Thy name forever more
> That hunger does not reach our door."

So, from my parents and grandparents, I learned both obedience and gratefulness.

As young mothers in our times keep vigil over their children, they must, of course, bear in mind that times have changed. In those days there was no danger of sending a little girl into the dark alone. It is different today when so much crime lurks in the shadows. New lessons must be found to emphasize the same truths, and it is the responsibility of individual homes to find the best and most effective way to teach truth so it bears fruit. Wrong is still wrong, and even the space age we live in cannot whitewash it. Only the truth can set us free.

February, to me, is a good month to start a little house-cleaning. It is as if the shelves and drawers cry out for attention. I like to do a couple of drawers and shelves a day. That way I can do them well, and it is a fun job, repaid by the pleasure I receive from seeing them neat. And I find myself wishing that all of them were done.

It is fine to have a system. A home is as important as any business firm and how smoothly would a business run if it did not have a system?

If we neglect our homes, we sin against them. There are so many things for a good housekeeper to do, but the chores can be fun. I feel as though I am playing a game, and every day I thank God for the privilege of being a homemaker. I think a home that is loved reflects a spirit of joy. And a very rewarding part of homemaking is planning the right foods for a family.

For February I have chosen some easy and inexpensive recipes which my *Mormor* might have served.

ENTREE

Crisply fried bacon and sausage	Potato patties
Lingonberries	Pickled cucumber

Hard tack (bread) and butter

DESSERT

Apple-*kaka* with vanilla sauce

Coffee or tea	Milk

POTATO PATTIES

1 egg	¼ teaspoon sugar
2 cups mashed potatoes	½ cup milk
¼ cup flour	2 tablespoons butter
½ teaspoon salt	

22

In a large bowl, stir the egg into the potatoes until the mixture is smooth. Add the flour, salt, sugar, and milk and stir well. Melt the butter in a frying pan. Drop heaping tablespoons of the mixture into the butter; fry until golden brown.

Place the potato patties on a large platter and heap the center of the dish with crisply fried bacon and sausage. Garnish with parsley.

SWEDISH PICKLED CUCUMBER

2 good-sized cucumbers
a dash of salt
½ cup sugar
white vinegar (enough to cover cucumbers)
2 tablespoons chopped parsley

Peel cucumbers and groove them by scraping them lengthwise with the prongs of a fork. Slice them thinly and place them in a deep plate covered with a smaller plate weighted with a heavy object. Let stand for four hours. Drain the water from the cucumbers and place them in a bowl. Sprinkle with the salt and sugar, and pour over them the white vinegar diluted with a little water. Mix and serve, sprinkled with chopped parsley.

Lingonberries can be purchased at almost any delicatessen or at a Swedish bakery.

APPLE-*KAKA*

2 cups crumbs of Vienna bread
1 cup butter
2 cups applesauce

Grate the two cups of crumbs from a two-day-old loaf of unsliced Vienna bread. Pack down firmly. Fry the crumbs in the butter. In a 9-inch pie plate alternate layers of crumbs and applesauce so that there are three layers of crumbs and two layers of applesauce. Bake in a moderate oven (350°) for 30 minutes. Serve warm topped with vanilla sauce.

VANILLA SAUCE

2 cups milk	1 egg yolk
¼ cup sugar	1 teaspoon vanilla
1 tablespoon potato flour	1 cup whipped cream

Place milk and sugar in a saucepan and bring to a boil. Thicken the mixture with the potato flour which has been stirred smooth in a little water. Bring again to a quick boil stirring constantly. Take the mixture from the stove and whip a slightly beaten egg yolk into it. Return mixture to the stove and stirring constantly, cook over low fire until it almost reaches the boiling point. Remove from the stove, stir in the vanilla and let cool. When the mixture is cool, fold in 1 cup of whipped cream and serve on the *kaka*.

Let every February be a happy month and serve lots of smiles with every meal.

GOLD NUGGET:

To keep fresh parsley crisp and green, place in a tightly covered glass jar and refrigerate. The parsley will keep for weeks.

∽3

Father God, we are grateful for each other and
for Thy protection and care. Grant us a deeper
understanding of how to live life to its utmost
so that we can be more useful each new day in
serving Thee and others. Amen.

To Mama the month of March was very
special. It was her biggest month for family birthdays. Mama had more people to remember in March than
in any other one month of the year except, of course, in
December. She possessed the gift of giving, a rare and
wonderful gift, so she loved every day of this month.
There were thirteen March birthdays in the family be-
sides her own, and there were also friends and shut-ins
whom she remembered with little gifts.

I often think birthdays mean more to our family than
to other people because as we brothers and sisters grew
up we were taught to regard them as something special.
And it was Mama who was the author of our birthday

joys. It was not the gifts or the years, but the atmosphere surrounding us that made each a day of days.

The celebration began early in the morning when everyone in the family, except the birthday child, would leave his bed. In the parsonage kitchen the big silver tray was set with an embroidered cloth, a cup and plate from the Sunday china, tall white candles in the silver candlesticks, and always some flowers in a low vase or perhaps a small plant. The hyacinth was Mama's favorite birthday plant, and in March there was always on the tray a hyacinth which filled the whole kitchen with a delicate fragrance, mingling with the smell of cardamom from the *kaka* which had been baked the day before.

The *kaka* was made of coffee-bread dough, filled with butter and jam and topped with finely chopped almonds decorating the celebrant's name and age which were written out on top. Then there were at least two kinds of cookies—perhaps spritz and *pepparkakor*. The *tårta* was not to be forgotten. This cake was traditional for each birthday in our home. It was a two-layer cake filled with applesauce and covered with whipped cream.

No one, not even royalty, could have been honored in a finer way, because this was the best that the household could give. And as the years went by and we grew up, were married, and had our own homes, the birthday celebration followed us like a sacred tradition and some of it has spilled over into the lives of our own children, who fuss for their little ones and make a birthday morning the happiest day of the year.

Looking back now I can see us all there in that kitchen on a March morning when the first of our family birthdays came. That one belonged to my sister Ann. (In Sweden we called her Anna-Lisa, which was her given name.) We all looked only half awake as we rubbed our eyes to get the sleep out of them. We were still dressed in our night clothes and had to keep absolute silence so that we would not awaken the birthday child. As soon as the coffee was ready, we formed the line—Mama first with the tray, then Papa with the *kaka* and *tårta* on another tray, then the children arranged according to age, each carrying his gift. What a sight it made! Each face glowed with a special radiance and as Mama struck up the tune, we all began to sing outside the door of the honored one. We always sang the same song which Mama had made up from one of her favorite hymns from the Baptist hymnal. She had just changed the words a little:

Tryggare kan ingen vara
än vår lilla Anna-Lisa rara
Stjärnan ej på himlafästed
Fågleln ej i kända nästet

Translated, the words that we sang said that no one could be safer than our little Anna-Lisa dearest, not the stars in the sky nor the birds in their nests. It was a lovely sentiment and we, as adults in our own homes, still sing that song. The new members of the family, even those who are not Swedish, have also learned the words and sing with us. Now, when we are scattered across the country, we sing it over the telephone or write it on cards or in letters. I think every family should have its own traditional song to pass along to the next generation.

Never, as long as I live, shall I forget the feeling of

being the birthday child and lying there in bed pretending to be asleep. But how could you sleep when there were butterflies in your stomach and you waited and waited to hear the soft shuffling of feet coming toward your closed door and the subdued laughter of one of the youngest, followed by that "Sh-sh" from Mama. Then you could hear Mama start the song and the rest joining in. The door opened and the candlelight appeared in the darkness of the early morning; you could see the flowers and the tray of goodies and all your brothers and sisters so happy and excited. They propped you up with pillows and there you were, the most important person in the whole world, all because it was your very own birthday, and everyone was happy that you had been born. There was so much love and admiration in the eyes of all your dear ones and the words were so warm and true: "Happy Birthday!" or in Swedish: "*Vi har den äran att gratulera!*"

After the coffee party, when one was stuffed with all the goodies he could eat, the gifts were opened. They were never expensive items, but they had been chosen with love. What a morning! And the joys kept up all day. They never let you forget that you were special. You were excused from the daily chores and waited on a little. Mama would make the meals special with a white tablecloth and real linen napkins. Nothing was too good for the child who was having a birthday.

When we were small, Mama would take time to sit down and tell us stories about the things that happened when we were tiny babies and how our names were chosen. Yes, on birthdays we were spoiled and pampered and loved and celebrated and that is something one never forgets. Life is short and divided into years, months, weeks, and days. It is not selfish, Mama explained, to take one day a year for one's self and make it very, very special. All this adds so much to the happiness in a home and makes its heart warm and glad.

I often wonder how Mama could give all those gifts to everyone on all those birthdays, but she did. She never forgot. When she was older, we used to beg her to stop.

"Just a card will be enough," we would say.

But Mama would not listen. To give was her greatest joy.

"As long as I live," she would say, her lovely blue eyes shining, "I shall be grateful for the gift of giving, and as long as God gives me years, I will give my small gifts as a token of all that has been given to me."

And Mama did.

Of course, we often had parties, too. Friends and their children dropped in during the afternoon for refreshment and there were games and fun and laughter. The birthday never ended until it was nighttime and we, so happy and content with our perfect day, would put our arms around Mama and Papa and whisper, "Thank you, thank you for the most wonderful birthday ever!"

And Papa would say, "Don't forget to thank God, too, before you go to sleep."

And that ended our special day.

March is a strange month, a fickle month! You can't trust it. One day the sun will shine so warmly on the earth that you feel sure spring has come; the next morning when you awaken, winter has returned. The wind is blowing, the snow is knee-deep, and the world is frozen and cold. Again the temperature rises and water floods everything. That night it freezes to glare ice on the sidewalks; then rain comes and it is cold and damp and it looks as if spring has forgotten to come back. But the sun peeps out some morning and smiles at our foolishness because it knows that now nature is really finished with snow and ice. There is something in the air that makes you feel as if you could turn somersaults of joy, for now the sun really means business and before we know it, April will appear with tulips and crocuses and the lawn will begin to turn green. We, too, begin to come alive and turn our minds toward housecleaning that still awaits us.

In March it is wise to clean cupboards, and cabinets. The closets need a good airing and all the clothes need to be hung on the line in the backyard. I like to do all the ceilings with a vacuum cleaner one week in March and strike that from my list of undone things. If there are lights in the ceiling, they need special attention. It is strange how dust will gather everywhere, and in the spring we have to go to war against it.

Lent usually comes in March, too, with Easter on its way. Some people make this a spiritual time in their lives. They give up little things for the sake of that inner voice which urges them to sacrifice as a token of love to God who gave His all for mankind. Others may concentrate on reading the Bible or various spiritual books—studying, meditating, and worshiping in special services at church. This is good, but shouldn't it be a part of our daily lives every month of the year? Certainly then we would find more value in our religion. God does not set aside a small period of time to be good to us; His goodness fills every day of the year.

This year, as I am writing this book, Easter comes early, in March. I like to decorate my home a little for this holiday, not as elaborately as I do at Christmas time, but just enough to create a springlike atmosphere. Colored eggs, daffodils, and pussy willows are a part of this season, and fluffy yellow chickens and shy rabbits stuck here and there make my home look festive. But these are not the real symbols of Easter. Crosses and angels remind us of the true spirit of this holy day. And how much we need to be reminded! The cross represents the greatest drama ever played on this earth, and its meaning is just as real today as it was two thousand years ago. It stands for the forgiveness of our sins, for salvation, and for the hope of eternal life. It stands for a forgotten past and a new beginning; also for humility and repentance. Angels remind us of that blessed morning when the stone was rolled away from the grave. They stand for hope and joy and laughter and light. Because He lived, we, too, shall live for ever and ever.

Yes, Easter is a magnificent holy day, so let us give it its proper place in our homes. Signs and tokens provide constant reminders to us in these busy times. Somewhere in the home there should be a Bible open to the story of that first Easter morning. The family should sit down and read that story together. If that is done every Easter, it will engrave itself deeply into the hearts of the children, and they will never forget the meaning it has for our world today. Perhaps beside the Bible on that table should stand, in its beauty and purity, a lovely white Easter lily.

When my girls were growing up, we prepared for the joy of Easter by keeping the hours from twelve to three on Good Friday as a sacred time. They never asked to play during those hours, nor did I ever shop or clean then. We sat together in the living room and meditated on the happenings of that first Good Friday, its meaning, and how it led to the joyousness of Easter morning. I wanted to teach them its significance as my parents had taught me.

The Jewish people know the importance of teaching their young the meaning of their faith. This is especially evident when they celebrate Passover. They relate to their children every event of that night when the angel of death passed over the Israelites enslaved in the land of Egypt. So it has been done from generation to generation. Should not we of the Christian faith do as much for our children, relating the story of our risen Lord? Things impressed on the minds of children when they are young will never be lost or forgotten. It is good to go to church often during that Easter week and especially for the family to sit together on Easter Sunday and sing "He lives! He lives! . . . He lives within my heart."

As I plan menus for the month of March, I can't help thinking of something that goes with those cold days when the strong wind tosses the tree branches and chills people to the bone. What can be better on a day like this than homemade pea soup and Swedish pancakes, or *plättar*, as we always called them!

Mama always served pea soup and *plättar* on Thursdays, and how we children looked forward to that meal! It was a fun meal for us. After we had eaten our soup, which always had plenty of chunks of lean ham in it, we stood in a line and waited for our pile of pancakes. There are seven round sections in a *plätt-panna* (a special pan for making *plättar*, available in a Swedish store or bakery), and Mama placed the finished pancakes in little piles on a big round platter. We each had one pile at a time. After one pile was gone, we would return for another. Mama never had time to sit down during that meal; she just stood there making those delicious little pancakes so we could eat as many as we wanted.

I find myself doing the same thing, since *plättar* should be eaten just as soon as they come out of the pan. It's fun to make them. Your hand must be light and quick when turning them over. They take just a minute to cook and need watching every second.

And when you eat your *plättar*, think of eight children standing in line refilling their plates over and over again and of a Mama who was never too tired to make as many as her little ones could eat.

ENTREE

Pea soup with ham chunks
Swedish *plättar* with lingonberries
Milk   Coffee

PEA SOUP

1 meaty ham bone
3 quarts and 1 pint of water
1 lb. of yellow dried peas
1 onion
  salt to taste

Remove the meat from the ham bone and reserve for later use. Place the bone in a large kettle. Add water, peas, and onion, and simmer until the peas are tender, about two to three hours. If the soup gets too thick, add more water. When ready to serve, place the ham chunks in the soup plate and pour the hot pea soup over them.

This makes quite a lot of soup, and it can be refrigerated for use a few days later. If preferred, it can be frozen.

SWEDISH *PLÄTTAR*

3 eggs	1 cup flour
⅓ cup sugar	2½ cups milk
1½ teaspoons salt	¼ pound butter (melted)

Beat the eggs, sugar, and salt together until smooth. Stir in flour, and beat in the milk, until smooth. Then add the melted butter and beat again. The mixture should be thin.

Fill the sections of the *plätt-panna* sparingly and tilt the pan to spread the mixture to fill the bottom of each section. Or, if a frying pan is used, mix with only 2 cups milk instead of 2½ cups. Be sure that the pan is tilted and turned so the mixture is spread out to form a large pancake. When the top of the mixture is dry and bubbly, turn the pancake quickly and lightly. The pancakes take just a few seconds to cook on each side.

Remove from the pan and place on a large platter (if made in a *plätt-panna*) or roll a large pancake on a knife and place on a platter. Put the platter over hot water to keep it hot. Serve with lingonberries, jam, syrup, or just sprinkled with sugar.

And for birthdays in March, here are the recipes for the birthday celebrations.

SWEDISH BIRTHDAY *KAKA*

First prepare a basic Swedish Coffee Bread Dough

5 cups flour	½ cup sugar
1 teaspoon ground carda- mom seed	1 teaspoon salt
	1 egg
1½ cups milk	2 packages yeast (dissolved
1 cup butter	in warm water)

Put flour in large bowl and add the cardamom seeds. Heat (do not boil) the milk and add shortening, sugar, and salt. Remove from the stove and let stand until lukewarm, then beat in the egg, using a beater, and add the yeast. Finally, add this to the flour and work the dough with your hand until it is smooth. When it no longer sticks to your hand, it has been worked enough. Sprinkle with flour and let it stand in a warm place, covered with a Turkish towel, until it has doubled its bulk.

To make the birthday-*kaka*, take a small part of the raised dough and roll out as you would a piecrust. Place in a deep pie plate of any size which has been greased and crumbed. Spread currant jelly (enough to cover) on top of the dough. Roll out a second pie-shaped piece of dough and place on top of the currant jelly. With your fingers, join the two layers of dough tightly together so that no jelly can leak out. Then roll a strip of dough into a long, thin piece and write the name of the birthday child (or adult) on the *kaka* and under the name write the age. For instance:

ANNA

16 YEARS OLD

Let the *kaka* rise until it is double in size. Brush it generously with melted butter and sprinkle it with coarse sugar (which can be bought in a Swedish bakery under the name of *Pearl-socker*) or grated loaf sugar. Then sprinkle with finely chopped almonds or other nutmeats.

Bake the *kaka* at 375° about 35 minutes or until nicely browned. Test with a toothpick. When the *kaka* is done, an inserted toothpick will come out clean. Remove from the oven and let it stand in the pan until cool. Remove the *kaka* from the pan carefully, using a spatula, and place on a plate. Cut into pie-shaped pieces.

To keep the *kaka* moist and fresh, cover with foil and keep in a cool place.

Use the remainder of the coffee-bread dough as follows:

Place the dough on a floured baking board and knead again until the dough is pliable. Form into desired shape—loaf, ring, or buns—and place on greased baking sheets. Let the dough rise again until it doubles its bulk. Bake in a 350° oven until golden brown (about 15 to 35 minutes, depending on the size of the bread).

TOPPING

Before baking, brush the dough with melted butter or a beaten egg yolk and sprinkle with coarse sugar and (optional) grated nuts.

TÅRTA

½ cup butter	2 teaspoons baking powder
1 cup sugar	½ teaspoon salt
3 eggs	1 cup milk
2 cups cake flour	1 teaspoon almond extract

Cream butter and sugar with an electric mixer, then add eggs, one at a time. Fold in the flour, baking powder and salt (which have been sifted together) alternately with the milk until the mixture is blended well. Add the flavoring. Pour into two 9-inch cake tins and bake at 350° for 18 to 25 minutes.

When the layers are completely cooled, spread applesauce between them and cover the entire cake with a thick layer of whipped cream.

SPRITZ COOKIES

½ pound butter
⅔ cup sugar
3 egg yolks
1 teaspoon almond extract
2½ cups flour

Cream butter and sugar together. Add the egg yolks and cream again until light and fluffy. Add the extract and then work in the flour a little at a time. Press the dough through a cookie press and shape into small rings or s's. Place on a buttered cookie sheet and bake in a 400° oven 10 to 15 minutes or until light brown. (Watch carefully as they burn easily.)

PEPPAR-KAKOR

1 cup dark corn syrup
1½ cups of sugar
½ pound butter
1 teaspoon ginger
½ teaspoon cinnamon
½ teaspoon cloves
1 tablespoon orange peel
¾ teaspoon baking soda
3 eggs
½ cup cream
1 teaspoon dry ammonia flour (bought in drugstore as Ammonia Bicarbonate)

Boil the first seven ingredients together. Let the mixture cool to lukewarm then add the baking soda which has been dissolved in a little warm water. Let the mixture cool and add eggs and cream. Then mix in enough flour to make the dough soft and pliable. Roll the dough out very thin on a baking board (a little at a time). Cut with a cooky cutter, and bake in a 375° oven about 10 to 15 minutes or until light brown. (Watch carefully.)

This recipe will make dozens of cookies which will keep for months if placed in a tightly covered container and kept in a cool place, or frozen.

As we look back at March, we realize that it has been a full, rich month and perhaps it has drawn the family closer together. It is good for a family to read together—perhaps one member reading aloud to the others. But the material should be an article or book that will interest everyone and which will inspire conversation. Such a time of togetherness, of sharing draws the family close.

GOLD NUGGET:
If you have a chunk of brown sugar which has become too hard to handle, grate it and it will be the right consistency again.

4

Dear Lord, for the happiness of young lives we pray, especially for each new bride-to-be. May they be big enough to know that there are burdens mixed with happiness and that they must bear them bravely. May they remember that a soft answer turns away an argument, and that to receive love, they must give it freely from an unselfish heart. Be Thou, O God, their guiding light, we pray. Amen.

AND so April finally comes! The weather in this month is never really dependable though. Even if sunshine floods the earth, the change can come suddenly, without warning, into rain, wind, cold, and—yes —even a snowstorm. But we know now that the snow will vanish as quickly as it came and the miracle of God's nature will begin to take place around us. There is a stirring in the dark earth—a moving and a peeping of all kinds of living things that will come up as grass, flowers, and plants.

The birds will begin to build their nests and from the way they chatter, we understand that at times they, too, have a hard time agreeing on just where the home nest should be. But soon they are busy carrying straw and other materials which are so essential to their happiness, and one day the mother bird lays her eggs.

This month is filled with living and planning and doing. And housewives, too, like to finish up the last of their housecleaning and to see that all is in order for the approaching warm weather, and that crisp clean curtains show from behind the shining window panes.

If I had the chance to live my life over and again to choose the month of my wedding, I think I would choose lovely April—not that our month of June wasn't nice, but I think April is even lovelier. There is a mystery about it that whispers and sings like a love song. April is that special.

I can remember that long ago, when I was a teen-ager, and Papa and I talked about death I asked him a strange question.

"Papa," I said, "if you could choose that month in which you must die, which one would you choose?"

Papa looked out through the open window onto the lake where the sun was dancing on the blue water, and he replied, "I think I would choose April—perhaps because at that time everything, even the dark earth, seems to be coming alive."

I was dismayed.

"Oh, Papa, I wouldn't want to die in the spring. That's the time when I really would want to live."

Papa did not die in the spring. He left us in the fall just

when summer was dying, but I often think of his words when spring comes.

Spring, in Sweden, is the most beautiful season. The American spring comes and goes too quickly. In my homeland the season comes slowly and every day the twilight lingers a bit longer, as if the light has to wrestle with the powers of darkness; at the same time it treads the earth with gentleness and care.

To have a garden in the springtime is a special blessing. There is a breathless wonder in finding the first bud of the year or seeing the first robin. And this excitement never comes again until the next April.

As I think back on Aprils of long, long ago, there is one bittersweet memory. It's a tragic tale, but life is a mixture of sun and shadows, of joy and tears. And from this tragedy I learned a lesson that helped me a great deal during those teen years when I, like so many other young girls, fell in and out of love. I learned never to play with hearts, and I know I tried to be careful, remembering what can happen when young love is spiteful.

I was a romantic girl of sixteen, and at that time life appeared to be a beautiful fairyland created just to allow me to partake of its joys to my heart's content.

There was a lovely park in our town where we young people used to meet on special nights when the orchestra was playing. Many lovers found their way to the hidden paths, carried away by the music and moonlight in the soft spring night. Sometimes I saw the glances exchanged by those in love and the happiness that shone from their faces as they walked hand in hand.

The particular couple I remember were so right for

each other. He was tall, blond, and handsome, dressed in the light gray Swedish military uniform with shining brass buttons and a three-cornered hat. She was dark and petite with the widest blue eyes I had ever seen, eyes always filled with fun and mischief. To me, they seemed the luckiest, happiest couple in the whole world. Perhaps, because everything was so perfect, the sudden end of their happiness hit me so hard.

She was a flirt, people said. Those lovely eyes held young men spellbound and she enjoyed flashing them whenever men folk were around. Her young man did not like this at all, and since he had leave only on week ends, he began to mistrust her. Then one night in the park they had an argument; many of us heard them. It was a beautiful April night when she walked away from him. And he never took one step to follow her or even to call her back. He just stood there sadly looking after her.

She lost no time finding another escort, and there she walked arm in arm with him deliberately seeking the path she knew the young soldier would take. Even now as I think about it, my heart cries a little. Love can be so cruel and thoughtless.

When the week end was over, he returned to the military base without talking to her, and she had made no sign of seeking his company.

On the following Monday morning he dressed and shaved and polished his gun, according to the rules; but instead of going to the mess hall for his breakfast, he stayed in the barracks. And there they had found him, sitting on his bed, leaning against the wall. On the floor was the gun, still pointed at him. He had pulled the trigger with his foot, and his young life, still so full of promise, had ended.

When the news reached our village, it spread like wildfire. But it affected us young people the most because we had known him so well. When we saw what it did to her, we could not judge her; there was only pity in our hearts. She really had not meant to leave him for good; she was just playing a game to teach him a lesson, to show that she was still young and free.

The Sunday they buried him we all stood there in the April sunshine, void of tears or words, but with that deeply painful hurt in our hearts that only the young can feel. We learned a lesson in life that day, and perhaps it made all of us better youngsters. We understood that he had been hasty and foolish; but also that love, the strongest force in the world, can be shattered as easily as the finest bone china when misused. Now each year, when April returns, I send up a little prayer for all young people that they will seek the wisdom to know that, when they fall in love, they have touched something borrowed from eternity, something which must be handled gently if it is to stay in their hearts for a lifetime.

But love also brings happier moments. And this lovely month brings no more joyous occasions than showers for brides-to-be. What fun for a home that can celebrate this kind of festivity, especially as a surprise for the honored guest. We have had many showers in our home; that is a dividend one gets when bringing up girls. One particular shower stands out in my memory. Although it was not an April shower, it was one of the most perfect ever given.

My younger daughter was having a bridal shower for

Susan, one of her best friends, and, of course, she let me get my hands into the whole thing. Everything was working out fine, except that Susan was determined never to be surprised, which made Carolyn want to surprise her more than ever. But how?

"Leave it to me," I said. "I have a plan in mind."

On the night we had chosen for the shower, Susan's mother had conveniently invited Carolyn to dinner, and the girls planned on going to a movie. Susan's parents were, supposedly, going out for the evening. Little did she know that her mother was to be a guest at Carolyn's house. Susan had been told that I was having a party that night and Carolyn had confided that she was glad to be out of the house when all my women friends descended in a group. So far, so good.

In our house everything was ready. The guests had all arrived on time. Cars were parked everywhere around the place, and just before the girls were to leave for the movie I called Susan's house.

Susan answered the phone, and I made my voice weak —almost a gasp: "Let me talk to Carolyn . . ."

I heard Susan calling Carolyn. Her voice was anxious. "It's your mother. She sounds terrible."

I spoke only a few words to Carolyn.

"Could you help me? I haven't stuffed the rolls yet. It would take just a few minutes if you and Susan could give me a hand . . ."

I knew that Carolyn was laughing on the inside, but that she would keep a straight face.

"Hang on, Mother, I'll ask Susan. Perhaps we can catch a later show."

44

I heard her tell Susan that I didn't feel well and that I needed help with the refreshments for all those ladies.

"Certainly we can help her," I heard Susan reply. "Your poor mother . . ."

They were there in no time at all. I opened the door, and Susan put her arms around me. "Don't worry, Mrs. Bjorn. Carolyn and I will take over. You don't have to do a thing. Just go and sit down."

Then someone started to play the wedding march. Although Susan must have heard the music, she never blinked an eyelash. Bless her! She was so concerned for me and my party that she hadn't even noticed all her friends, or even her own mother.

It was not until the crowd began to shout, "Surprise!" that she looked around. And there sat her mother and all her close friends. Susan's eyes just got bigger and bigger; then suddenly she just collapsed in my arms. I assure you that never was there a more surprised bride-to-be. And what fun it had been to plan it all and be successful.

Decorating for the shower is the most fun, I think. There are many ways of doing this, but I prefer to stick to the way we have done it for all the young brides— simple, but lovely. There is a special chair for the honored guest near a pink umbrella trimmed with cascading streamers and fresh flowers and a cluster of large white wedding bells. A clothes basket covered with pink crepe paper is perfect for small packages; the larger ones with their lovely gift wrapping and fancy ribbons can be placed here and there to add to the decorations.

The table, too, must be beautiful. A net cloth over soft pink taffeta makes a very effective base for a centerpiece of fresh flowers in a low vase and four tall, pink candles in silver candlesticks. Pink shower napkins are laid out by the plates and the cups are stacked at one end around the silver coffee service. There might even be a doll bride and groom, all lending a festive air.

The food, of course, will vary according to the taste of the hostess. I love lots of good things to eat, and I love to prepare them. Here then is a sample menu of what I would serve.

I would have tiny finger rolls filled with lobster, chicken, and tuna salad, arranged on a large silver platter. There would also be dainty open-faced sandwiches of cream cheese and nuts, cucumber and parsley, or deviled ham and pickle slices, cut in hearts or rings. To accompany these would be baby gherkin pickles and large ripe and green olives, and of course a large bowl of potato chips. Then there would be a large Swedish *klippkrans* cut in thin slices, and for cookies there would be kisses, chocolate wafers, and pecan tarts topped with whipped cream.

KLIPPKRANS

Use the basic coffee-bread dough which has risen once. Take as much as you need to make a large ring. Roll the dough out flat like cookie dough and spread with ½ pound butter and ½ cup sugar. Roll the dough into a long roll and form into a large ring. Place on a greased cookie sheet or round broiler pan. With a pair of scissors snip deep gashes in the ring, and crisscross alternating pieces over each other like a braid. Let the dough rise to double its size, then brush with a beaten egg and sprinkle with slivered almonds and coarse sugar. Bake at 350° for 35 to 40 minutes, depending on the size of the ring. After

30 minutes, watch the ring carefully. When done, it should be golden brown; and a toothpick, inserted into it, should come out clean. Cool before removing from the pan.

KISSES

4 egg whites
1 cup sugar
1 tablespoon lemon juice

Beat the egg whites until they form stiff peaks. Beat in ⅔ cup of sugar and add lemon juice. Fold in the remaining sugar lightly.

Drop by the spoonful onto a greased baking sheet (or a sheet covered with aluminum foil). Bake in a 250° oven for 1 hour. Turn the heat off and let the kisses stand in the oven until cool. Remove from baking sheet and store in an air-tight container, preferably one with a screw top.

The kisses *should not be brown;* they should be white. If they start to brown, turn the heat way down.

CHOCOLATE WAFERS

½ cup butter
1 cup sugar
2 eggs (beaten)
2 squares baking chocolate (melted)
¼ teaspoon salt

¼ teaspoon vanilla
⅔ cup flour
1 cup chopped nut meats (mixed with 1 teaspoon flour)

In a bowl, cream butter, add sugar, and then add the beaten eggs. Next add melted chocolate, salt, and vanilla. Cream together until smooth. Work in flour, a little at a time. Last add the nut meats.

Drop with a teaspoon onto a greased baking sheet. Place a piece of nut on each wafer. Bake at 350° for 10 to 15 minutes. After 10 minutes, watch wafers as they burn easily. They should be dry and puffed when ready. Cool on baking sheet before removing.

PECAN TARTS

Shell

½ pound butter
2 3-ounce packages of cream cheese
2 cups flour

Cream butter until fluffy. Add cream cheese and work until smooth. Mix in the flour a little at a time. Take walnut-size portions and press into tiny muffin pans, forming a shell and making sure it is not too thick. Into each cup put the filling.

FILLING

3 eggs (slightly beaten with fork)
1½ cups brown sugar
1 cup white sugar
2 teaspoons vanilla
¾ cup finely chopped pecans

Mix all the ingredients together until well blended. Put 1 teaspoon in each shell. Bake at 350° for 20 to 25 minutes. Let cool completely. Before serving top with colored (optional) whipped cream.

It isn't really necessary to plan entertainment for a shower, since the opening of the gifts takes up most of the time. But it is nice to have something for the guests to look at while they wait. Often I have made scrapbooks for the bride-to-be, showing her life from her birth to her engagement. This is done by cutting appropriate pictures from magazines to represent the high points of her life and captioning them. It's fun for the guests to look at, and it makes a fond keepsake for the bride.

And it would not be a complete shower if we did not say a prayer in our hearts for the future of our happy bride, for she is going into a new world where she will have to make many adjustments. And so much will depend on how she gets started.

Showers are great fun, but there are also practical tasks to be accomplished this month. At the end of April, all the woolen articles should be cleaned or washed before placing in plastic bags or a special drawer with mothballs. Furs should be hung in the sunshine and then placed in plastic bags, or better still, put into storage until fall. In the spring, clothes make a lot of difference to our morale. If we don't need new ones, the old can be given a new look by adding a ribbon, a flower, or a tuck here and there. Miracles can happen, even in our wardrobes, if we take the interest, time and patience.

And our meals for the month must be simple, such as Swedish meatballs with gravy.

ENTREE

Swedish meatballs
Baked potatoes with sour cream
French cut green beans with almonds
Lettuce with Russian dressing
Shredded-wheat bread and butter

DESSERT

Custard with Raspberries

Coffee   Milk

49

MEATBALLS

2 slices stale white bread
1 bouillon cube (dissolved in 1 cup boiling water)
1 pound ground chuck
1 egg (unbeaten)
1 small onion, finely chopped and fried in butter
¼ teaspoon white pepper
¼ teaspoon allspice
½ teaspoon salt

Soak bread in bouillon water. Add ground chuck and work until well mixed. Work in the egg, and add onion and spices. Work the mixture until it is smooth and pliable. If it feels dry, add more water.

Shape into fairly small meatballs and fry in butter until dark brown. They should be fried slowly, making sure they are well done. This takes about a half hour. Remove meatballs from frying pan and sprinkle 2 tablespoons of flour into the drippings. Stir over a low heat until brown. Add water and 2 tablespoons heavy cream and bouillon cube (or cubes) to taste. Strain and pour over meatballs.

FRENCH BEANS

Wash fresh green beans and slice lengthwise in thin slices. Place in salted water and cook for about ten minutes. When done, pour off water and season with ¼ teaspoon Accent, 1 tablespoon butter, salt, and a little pepper. Sprinkle with finely sliced almonds.

SHREDDED-WHEAT BREAD

2 shredded-wheat biscuits (large size)
2 cups boiling water
2 tablespoons butter
1 teaspoon salt
½ cup molasses

1 package yeast
4 level cups flour

Add boiling water to shredded wheat, butter, salt, and molasses. Let stand until lukewarm. Add yeast, which has been dissolved in a little warm water, add flour and work until well mixed. Place in two loaf pans which have been well greased, and cover with a Turkish towel. Let rise until double in bulk. Bake in a moderate oven (350°) for 45 minutes. Remove bread from oven and brush the tops of loaves with a little sugar water (1 teaspoon sugar to ¼ cup water). Let the bread cool in the baking pans.

CUSTARD

2 cups milk
2 eggs (slightly beaten)
¼ cup sugar
½ teaspoon salt
dash of nutmeg

Heat milk (*do not boil*). When hot, remove from stove and pour into mixing bowl. Let stand until lukewarm, then add slightly beaten eggs, sugar, and salt. Beat together for two minutes. Pour into greased custard cups and sprinkle with nutmeg. Place cups in a pan of water and bake in 250° oven (about 20 minutes) until a knife inserted into the custard comes out clean. Cool.

When ready to serve, remove custard from cups with a small spatula or knife, place on a plate, and top with raspberries (frozen or fresh) and a dab of whipped cream garnished with one raspberry.

Thus, another month has passed from our life into God's eternity. Let us think back on this fourth month and take stock of what we have done with our days. How much good have we left behind us in the world that will be a blessing to others?

GOLD NUGGET:

Open your eyes wide to the wonders of God's world in the springtime. Take time to stop and behold and listen though others pass by without seeing or hearing.

❧5

"Lord God," we thank Thee for flowers and birds' songs and spring rain and wind. For a home with a garden and a loved one who slips his hand in mine as we walk on the soft grass among our flowers, I say, "My cup runneth over." I have received so much and I worship Thee, Giver of all these things. Amen.

IT was in the month of May that we, as a family, left Sweden. Whenever I think of this beautiful month, I experience again that feeling which tugs at my heart and sends shivers down my spine—that feeling of not knowing what the future would hold. Only those who have permanently departed from their homeland can know the inner turmoil that fills a person, the confusion of pulling up one set of roots and putting down another.

At the time I was a teen-ager and filled with dreams which I had woven continually into my heart. How well I remember standing on the pier in Gothenburg. My wide unbelieving eyes stared at the enormous ship rising majestically out of the blue water. How very white she was and how very graceful! She looked to me like a giant, wingless swan. I was to live aboard that ship for almost two weeks, and day and night she would take me farther and farther from my homeland. It was the leaving that hurt, even though I would still be surrounded by my family. But Sweden was so very special to me and the love I had for her was so different from any other feeling in the world—a love that had been in my heart for as long as I could remember. In this land my ancestors slept in their graves in well-kept cemeteries. And there was one special grave in a small village by a beautiful lake where my dear *Mormor* rested. It was strange to feel so divided. The thoughts moving through my mind created a deep sadness; yet another part of me was happily excited, anticipating the newness of my future life. Then my eye caught sight of the flag on the ship's mast—the beautiful Swedish flag with its gold cross on a field of heavenly blue—as it waved gracefully and proudly in the sunshine. I would not see the gold on blue in America, for there another flag would wave. How would I ever be able to accept and honor it? And how could I love a new country? But anticipation and curiosity soon filled me with a sense of adventure.

What would my new country be like? What did the future hold for me? I was young and free and perhaps I would meet someone over there, who would be really special?

Then, as though disgusted with myself for thinking such frivolous thoughts, I promised that I would return to Sweden soon. I would not stay "over there" forever. As soon as I had grown up, I would come back here, for this really was my home.

Yes, even though many, many years have passed, I can still remember my thoughts on that seventh of May, 1924, and I know that they will always be a part of me until the end of my days on earth.

Days later, when we were far out on the ocean and saw land no more, I stood staring into the gray-green water and contemplating the tales told by others who had crossed these deep, stormy waters. I giggled a little as I thought of the one freshest in my memory. It was the story of a young girl I knew, who had crossed the ocean to join her fiancé who had gone to America a few years before. The story had been told to me by another girl who had accompanied her on the trip and had since been back to Sweden for a visit. She had gleefully reported the mishap that had taken place on this very ship; and although the event was really rather sad, I can't help but smile when I think of it. It seems that just before the young girl was to leave for America she had been plagued with a terrible toothache. She went to have it taken care of, but discovered, much to her horror, that all of her teeth had to be pulled. The dentist assured her that he could fit her with a set of false teeth, so that no one, not even her fiancé, would ever know. And he was right! Had it not been for a storm at sea, no one could have suspected. But, alas, nature intervened and changed the course of several lives. The night before the ship was to dock in New York there was a violent storm which upset the festivity of the Captain's dinner. It could have been the rocking of the

55

ship, or it could have been that she had eaten too much, but whatever the cause, the young girl became quite ill. And while she was losing her dinner over the railing that night, she also lost her beautiful, new set of teeth.

Never had there been a sadder young lady. What would she do? How could she meet her fiancé with a toothless smile? When the ship docked the next morning, she hid; instead of rushing into his arms, she ducked behind people and trunks until she could get to a taxi and find a hotel. Her bewildered fiancé searched the ship for her, anxiously asking other passengers if they knew of her whereabouts. He even wrote to her home, thinking perhaps that she had missed the boat altogether, but to no avail. Finally he must have given up, for he was not heard of again.

In the meantime, the girl found a job and worked until she had earned herself enough money to buy a brand-new set of teeth, all of which took time. Then, instead of setting out to find her fiancé, she discovered she had fallen in love with the son of the wealthy family for whom she worked as a maid, and that he had fallen in love with her. After a year she married him and settled down in New York City. No one ever knew what became of the fiancé, but I was told that she lived happily and never once regretted the lost teeth which changed her whole future. What a story that was!

We really traveled in luxury in the second class. I promptly fell in love with the Chief Steward of our dining room, and every day of the voyage he sent to my stateroom a basket of fruit which I had to share with Papa, who insisted that it was really meant for him. I did not dare protest for fear of being watched for the rest of the trip.

Yes, May brings many memories! And it is pleasant now to sit in our lovely garden and think back. And in the twilight when the stars begin to light the sky, I bless my adopted land. I say to myself, "I love America. It is my country now and the beautiful Star-Spangled Banner is my flag." This is the wonder of it all—that, as the years go by, we who came from other countries, heartsick at leaving our homelands, dig our roots deep into American soil, transferring our love to our new land.

America has given me so much. It has made my dream come true, showering me with honor and recognition. I want to live here always, and when my time comes, I'd like to die here. Strange how it has happened! But it has! I still love Sweden and always shall, but this is my country now. It has both my citizenship and my heart. So in the soft loveliness of spring I bless this month which brought me here.

May is the time of apple blossoms, lilacs, tulips, dogwood, and so many, many beautiful things that my heart says a continual thank you to God for creating such a wonderful world. I love our garden and in this month I enjoy getting out early in the morning to work in it before the sun gets too warm. A garden on a May morning is something special. The air is so fresh and pure—neither too cool nor too warm. It is just right. The birds' songs have a lilt belonging to spring alone. There is excitement and happiness everywhere. I believe the heart of the home beats with joy in May, that the whole house is filled with an atmosphere of fun and togetherness.

With our spring cleaning done, we housewives have time to poke around in the garden, but there are still a few little household tasks to attend to. The beds must have attention. Pillows need to be given a good shaking and hung on the clothesline; and so do quilts and unwashable bedspreads. Blankets and mattress pads should be washed, and instead of placing them in the dryer, get them out in the sunshine. There is nothing that smells better than a blanket which has been dried in the sun. Mattresses should be vacuumed, and given a good airing with all the windows left open. They need to be turned, too, so they don't become worn in one spot. Inner springs are easy to clean, but the coil springs take much more time. But how good it is to get the bed dust out of them —making all the bedding fresh and clean. Washable bedspreads should be taken care of too, so that everything is fresh and clean.

Then the time is ours to spend on those extra things we like to do. Perhaps our reading has lagged a bit. How important it is to read new books and articles, to keep up with the world and with local happenings. Reading is food for the mind; to keep it alert and informed is to keep it healthy.

But let us never forget to feed our souls, too. In May we can drink in the beauty of the world around us and think of our Creator. We can worship walking in the garden, sitting by a lake, just looking up at the blue sky and feeling the wonderful sunshine warm our bodies. Perhaps the soft spring rain caressing our faces as we lift them toward heaven will melt away any resentment and malice within our hearts. There is something very refreshing about the spring showers and, after they are over, everything is so much greener and purer. Thank God for the rain!

And let us take time in May to think of all our blessings. There are so many people who are on sick beds and in institutions of all kinds, shut away from joy and sunlight and gardens. Let us take time to give of ourselves; to drop in at the hospitals and nursing homes; to cheer the old and the lonely; to bring a bouquet of spring flowers, a book, or some fruit. Surprisingly enough it will make you even happier than the one you visit. It is a good way to show gratefulness for the health and happiness so freely given to us.

One of my spring hobbies is my garden. I can't expect every one to be as enthused about gardening as I am, but to be outside and feel the soil in my hands, to weed, to plant, and to see that flowers and shrubs have the right kind of nourishment is like a good dose of vitamins to me. When I am alone, I talk to my flowers. I tell them they are beautiful and sometimes when I walk by my lovely dogwood I whisper, "God bless you!" I believe that trees, flowers, and plants can feel and hear. No geraniums ever blossomed more beautifully or grew more profusely than those on my Mama's window sill.

Her friends used to say to her, "Maria, how can your geraniums blossom like that all the time?"

Mama used to smile happily and reply, "That is because I talk to them!"

So I practice Mama's method and it always works. I think everything alive longs for love and attention, and the more love we give to our gardens, the more they give back to us.

May is also a good month in which to just sit and relax, not even thinking, just drawing strength from the sun and the wind and the fresh air. At times we rush too much, we run too fast, we hustle and bustle and wear ourselves out. We need rest to keep our bodies strong and well; so in the month of May let us rest and we all will be so much happier because we took that time to do the right thing.

Our menu for May is in keeping with spring.

ENTREE

Salmon casserole

Deluxe carrots

Tossed salad with cheese

Dill pickles

Schnecken buns

DESSERT

Angel food delight

Coffee or tea   Milk

SALMON CASSEROLE

5 medium potatoes	1 teaspoon chopped parsley
1 pound can of red salmon	1 cup milk
salt and pepper to taste	breadcrumbs (flavored preferred)
1 egg (slightly beaten)	
1 tablespoon flour	3 tablespoons butter

Peel potatoes, slice thinly and place in salted water. Boil for two minutes. Skin and bone the salmon. Arrange the potatoes and salmon in layers in a buttered casserole dish, first a layer of potatoes, then a layer of salmon sprinkled with salt, pepper, and little chunks of butter; then potatoes, then the rest of the salmon, then the remaining potatoes. Salt again sparingly.

In a separate bowl, mix the egg, milk, flour, and parsley. Pour this mixture over the potatoes and salmon, making sure it covers the whole casserole. Top with flavored breadcrumbs and dabs of butter.

Bake in a 325° oven for 35 minutes. Serve with melted butter. This should make four generous servings.

DELUXE CARROTS

Peel carrots and cut lengthwise into tiny strips. Place in salted water and boil until tender. Remove from heat, drain, and pour two tablespoons orange juice over the carrots. Season with butter, salt, and Accent.

TOSSED SALAD

In one bowl place cut-up lettuce, celery, green pepper and a few slices Bermuda onion. Toss lightly. In another bowl place cut-up tomatoes, radishes, cucumber, and a few slices of sharp cheddar cheese. Mix. Just before serving combine the contents of both bowls, toss lightly, season with salt, freshly ground pepper, and Accent. Add French dressing and serve.

SCHNECKEN BUNS

2 packages yeast
1 cup warm (not hot) water
1 cup sugar
1 cup butter

1 teaspoon salt
1 cup boiling water
2 eggs (slightly beaten)
6½ cups flour

Dissolve the yeast in warm water. In a large mixing bowl combine sugar, butter, and salt. Add boiling water. Stir until the butter is melted. Cool to lukewarm. Add the eggs and dissolved yeast. Mix well. Add four cups of the flour; beat until smooth. Work in the rest of the flour gradually, beating the dough well. Chill for at least four hours. Divide dough in half. Roll each half on a lightly floured surface into 18x10 inch rectangles.

FILLING

2 cups light brown sugar (firmly packed)
1½ teaspoons cinnamon
¾ cup melted butter
1 cup seedless raisins
1 cup chopped nuts
melted butter

Combine brown sugar, cinnamon, and the ¾ cup melted butter. Sprinkle ¼ of the mixture over each of the rectangles, and sprinkle each with ½ cup raisins and ½ cup nuts. Starting with the long side, roll jelly-roll fashion. Slice into two dozen 1½ inch rounds.

Sprinkle the remaining filling into the bottom of 3-inch muffin pans. Place the sliced rounds in the pans. Cover with Turkish towel. Let rise in a warm place until double in bulk, about 1¼ hours. Brush with melted butter.

Bake in 375° oven for 20 to 25 minutes. Remove from oven and turn upside down on a large tray immediately. Do not cool in tins.

ANGEL FOOD DELIGHT

1 angel food cake
2 packages frozen (or fresh) raspberries
1 pint whipping cream

Slice the angel food cake into three layers. Cut away some of the inside of the cake.

Drain the raspberries. Save juice. Whip the cream.

Spread the whipped cream on each layer and sprinkle with raspberries. Put the layers together. Mix some of the raspberries in the whipped cream and fill in the cut-away section. Then frost the entire cake with whipped cream and sprinkle with raspberries.

SAUCE

juice from 2 packages frozen raspberries
1 cup water
1 tablespoon cornstarch or 1 teaspoon potato flour
1 teaspoon lemon juice

Dilute the raspberry juice with the water. If you use cornstarch, put it in when *juice is boiling*. If you use potato flour, put it in while *juice is still cold;* then bring to a boil. (Potato flour makes the sauce bright red. Cornstarch makes it cloudy.) Flavor with lemon juice. Cool sauce and serve with cake.

It is especially pretty served from a glass dish with a silver ladle.

I like to have a big bouquet of lilacs on the table in May, although they make me a little nostalgic. They bring back memories of how our beautiful parsonage in Sweden was taken apart, the furniture sold or given away, and everything dear and lovely destroyed. We had to put our home together again in a new country. It was a strange country, so different from what we knew, and our hearts were still homesick. But the first time we sat down to eat in our new home, there on the table stood a large bouquet of purple and white lilacs, just like the ones that grew in our garden in Sweden. They told us gently that much would still be the same because God's flowers bloomed in America, too, and in my heart I blessed the lilacs. They are still dear to me today, tying together my two countries

63

with a fragrance belonging only to springtime. Thank God for lilacs!

GOLD NUGGET:
Fruit stains will come out of linen easily if they are dipped into boiling water.

∽6

Dear God, thank you for years so crowded with the fullness of life. Thank you for the mountains and their grandeur that make us feel our own smallness as we worship a Great God. We are grateful for our loved ones, children, grandchildren, and sons-through-love, now a part of our family. Our hearts can hardly contain it all and on this, one of the most beautiful mornings of our lives, we worship and love and honor Thy Holy Name. Amen.

June is our month! Every married couple has a month that is their own—the month in which they were married. So June belongs to Bob and me. It was in that month that we made our home together and began to live with each other for as many years as God would give us here on earth.

I shall never forget the eagerness and joy that filled my heart as we found that first apartment, bought our own furniture, and placed each piece in its own special position. Everything had been paid for in cash, and while our bank account was meager, what we had was ours.

What a busy time it was as I helped Mama plan and prepare for the big wedding. Looking back, I can see that it was a big wedding only because our church was so small that if we had one hundred people there, it would be filled to capacity. Even so Mama and I pondered over whether or not we dared invite one more family, and if we did, where we would seat them.

My heart was bubbling over like a springtime brook rushing down the mountainside. The feeling was too big for words, but I shall never forget it. It was exciting to think that my own Papa would be the minister to marry us and that my handsome eldest brother would walk up the aisle with me to give me away.

Our wedding ceremony was part Swedish and part English. Mama had draped two big stuffed chairs in white, and Bob and I, instead of walking back down the aisle after we had been married, walked to those chairs placed at the front of the church. There we were seated to listen to the program given in our honor. There were solos sung and music played and poems read which had been written just for us and telegrams from loved ones in Sweden and from friends all over America were read aloud. After the program was finished, there was a receiving line and then refreshments were served. Here Mama had outdone herself with fancy pastries, cookies, and cakes. Our wedding was different from any I have ever attended, but it was lovely. A wedding does not have to follow a standard pattern, for every couple has a right to plan their own just the way they would like it.

Our honeymoon was short, but they were lovely, happy, sunshiny days. When it was over, we were both eager to return home . . . to our own home which was waiting to receive us. Perhaps the greatest moment of my life was the one when I walked through that door. Inside we knelt in silence for a moment, asking God for His blessing over our life together.

It takes two to make a marriage, but individually each can do so much to keep it filled with love and peace. Two who have come from different backgrounds, perhaps even lived in worlds apart, become as one. It takes a melting down of wills, a cheerful willingness to go a little more than halfway both in giving in and in planning for the future. The key of diplomacy is very useful in married life. If handled carefully, it will fit the lock of any door that has been bolted shut.

I know that both my husband and I have learned a lot about each other through the years. We compromise in things which could cause trouble, and each tries not to force the other into his or her own set pattern. My Bob hates to walk. I love to take long walks hand in hand with my fine husband, and he walks with me many times even though he is tired. I love musicals, but Bob likes funny movies or plays where he can do a lot of laughing. So at times I sit through that kind of entertainment and he will go to a musical with me. I do many things that I don't like doing, and so does Bob, because we like to make each other happy.

It seems strange to me that marriage is the one position we can take without previous training or preparation. It is the highest and most important job one can hold and yet people rush into it blindly. To know something about each other should be part of the training. How does a girl feel about being a wife? Does she enjoy cooking, cleaning, and keeping house? What kind of mother will she make? A man should want to know his sweetheart's views on such things. And what kind of a father will he be? Perhaps every girl should know that when the honeymoon is over and real life begins, the attentive husband may disappear behind his newspaper both morning and evening. All men seem to enjoy reading at the wrong time. A young wife wants her husband's attention in the morning and especially when he returns from work. She is hungry for his companionship; she is anxious to tell him about her day, and most of all, she wants to hear that he loves her. But he is tired after a busy day. He relaxes behind his newspaper and the words she is waiting for are not spoken.

A wise woman will sit down and analyze the situation. Is this such a terrible thing her husband is doing? Why does it annoy her so much? Why not just let him be himself and read the paper to his heart's content? He will love her even more for this freedom. When he is through reading, he will be his attentive, happy self again, perhaps even more so because there is no tension. This is just one of the little pet peeves that ruins so many homes in our day. Oh, there must be similar things that irritate a husband—perhaps a wife who doesn't bother to look her best in the morning. It would take only a few minutes to brush her hair and make herself presentable. Although I can't see things completely from a man's viewpoint, I know that it's up to each wife to discover the source of any irritation that lets the little "fox" slip into the home. It is the little foxes that spoil the vineyard, the Bible says. But if both husband and wife watch out for them, they will never get inside the door.

The way a marriage starts off is most important. If homes are solid, the nation is solid, and the nations form the whole world. So what we do in our individual home affects the whole world.

Becoming parents is the next step. Parents who bring up their children to be fine, upright citizens give a valuable gift to the next generation, a gift that is priceless. There should be much fun and laughter in a home. And when there is peace and love there, children grow up secure and strong enough to meet life's problems. They unconsciously form their own pattern from their daily life. To earn respect from their children, a husband and wife must show respect for each other, and blessed are the children whose parents know this.

It is good for children to learn to believe in life and their fellow men, and most of all, in God as the Creator of heaven and earth. This gives them a sense of security and stability. And I think that children should be free to believe that miracles do happen.

Every household makes its mistakes, and there are many things we older parents would do differently if we could live life over with the wisdom the years have given us. But there is one thing I have never regretted—that our girls could live in a make-believe world if they wanted to. I never tried to stop them from believing that anything could happen if they but put on magic shoes and slipped into an invisible cloak.

When our Shirley was about four years old, she suddenly showed a great desire to help me plant my garden.

I gave her a package of radish seeds. "Darling, put these in the dark earth," I said as she spilled them out into her little hand. "All these tiny seeds have life in them, given to them by God. If you plant them, water them, and love them, they'll begin to grow and one day you'll pull up round, red radishes, and we can have them for dinner."

She looked curiously at the seeds.

"Mine will grow very fast, Mommy," she assured me. "They'll grow so fast that we can have radishes from my garden tomorrow night."

I looked down at that eager face—so sure, so confident, with not a shadow of a doubt in the bright blue eyes. At first I thought that I must explain to her that this could not happen, but on a second thought I decided to let it go. Why not let her be happy until life, in its own time, taught her the lesson of patience? Tomorrow there would be no radishes to pull and that would be time enough to explain things the right way.

That night before Shirley went to bed, she ran out into her garden patch and I watched her there, in her pink bathrobe, kneeling on the ground. The kitchen window was open and I listened.

"Dear God," she prayed, "let my radishes grow quickly so that we can have some for dinner tomorrow night. Amen."

My heart ached a little as I tucked her into bed that night. It would be hard to see her disappointed on the morrow. But it just had to be—that was all.

The next morning, before I had even had time to think,

she was out in the garden again. Now she will know, I thought, as I busied myself fixing breakfast. Then suddenly there was a shout and the patter of tiny, running feet. The back door pushed open and there she stood holding the biggest, reddest bunch of radishes I had ever seen. I felt faint. I had to sit down. I rubbed my eyes, telling myself that I was dreaming.

"Where did you get those?" I finally blurted out.

"From my garden, where I planted them. They did grow fast, Mommy, and they are such pretty red ones. Now we can have them for dinner."

I walked out into the garden and stood there looking at her patch of ground. Sure enough, there were holes in the dirt where she had pulled each one. But . . . things like this just did not happen.

Mr. Smith's voice from next door brought back my sanity. He had come from his garden and was standing beside me.

"Did you ever see anything like it?" he asked with a twinkle in his eye. "Those radishes grew faster than anything I've ever seen."

Then Mrs. Smith came across the lawn to join us. "We heard little Shirley pray last night," Mrs. Smith explained. "It was such a cute, touching little scene that my husband decided to be God's helper. He went out and bought the biggest radishes he could find and just before dark, he planted them in Shirley's garden. We watched for her this morning, knowing very well she would be out there the first thing. Sure enough, she came, running across the lawn like a little elf, and she pulled out those radishes as though it were the most natural thing in the world for them to be there. It was certainly worth a little trouble. Someday, of course, you'll have to tell her the truth. But let her be happy for a while. A child's faith is so lovely."

I thanked them both, but I wondered about it. Even though I was thrilled at my daughter's happiness at the moment, someday she would know this wonderful thing was not true. It was years before I could tell her, and when I did, to my surprise, it did not hurt her or damage her faith in God. That miracle had been one of the biggest things in her young life and she looked at me calmly and said, "God did answer my prayer just the same, Mommy. He can use people to do His work if He wants to. He told Mr. Smith to see that my prayer was answered so that we could have radishes for dinner that next night."

She knows that, to be happy, her own children have to see magic take place, and many times she has astonished me with her wisdom. Once when I was visiting her in her home on Long Island, she had just painted her hallway wall going up the stairs a shiny white. I scolded her mildly.

"Don't you think it's foolish," I said, "to have a white wall like that with four youngsters running up and down those stairs? Just think what that white wall will look like with all their finger marks."

"Don't worry about it, Mother." She laughed. "I have that all figured out."

That afternoon when the children came home from school, she told them to wet their hands and go out into the garden and get them good and dirty. They were delighted. Next she had them walk up the staircase one by one and touch the wall. Never have I seen them obey more quickly. And there they were—finger marks all over the beautiful newly painted wall.

She's teaching them a lesson, I thought. Hereafter they'll be very careful because they themselves have seen how badly it looks. But that was not the idea at all.

The next morning I slept a bit late. When I awoke, I was immediately conscious of the odor of fresh paint. And as I started down the stairs, I stopped in wonder and amazement. I could hardly believe my eyes. My daughter had been up early, painting again, but this time she had painted in various bright colors every finger mark that the children had made. It was the most beautiful decoration I had ever seen and to me the dearest. Sometimes mothers can't keep up with their clever daughters, and I had never been more pleased or surprised at her handling of a delicate situation. The marks will be there for years, and as the children grow older, the reminder will be more and more treasured, for it represents the pure gold of a mother's heart.

My older daughter is unique in many ways. There was a time when her furniture began to show signs of wear. There were holes in the divan covering and on the living-room chairs, but she was not quite ready to replace them.

"We'll wait until the children are a little older," Shirley said as we stood together, viewing the hardly presentable living-room furniture.

The next time I visited, the same furniture was still there, but with a different look. Now there were bandages over every tear, hole, and scratch.

"Oh, Shirley, what in the world is all this?" I laughed.

"I've never seen a more ridiculous looking living-room set. Do you mean to tell me you're going to keep the bandages on them like that?"

"Yes, for a while, until we get new furniture," she answered with that little lilt which comes into her voice when she thinks she's outsmarted me. "You see, Mother, our furniture is sick and this is the way we're telling the world. Now instead of feeling embarrassed about it, it is the best conversation piece we've ever had in the house. And the kids just love to have their friends come in to look at our sick furniture. It really has helped our morale in this critical time."

Well, it was very clever indeed, but the sick furniture found compassion in my heart and it was not long before they had a brand-new set. Sometimes mothers have to step in and help in a sickroom. That was one of those times when it was a joy to lend a hand.

This year my husband and I celebrated our fortieth wedding day! How wonderful to have so many years behind us. We did not want a party this time. Instead we took a little trip to the White Mountains in New Hampshire, driving over many of the roads we had driven along forty years before on our first honeymoon. We found a lovely old New England inn in the midst of the mountains where the most delicious food was served and where we could rest and relive the years we had spent together as husband and wife. Early on our day, June eleventh, a beautiful Sunday morning, we drove down the mountain road. As we stood there at Crawford Notch in the still-

74

ness of the Sabbath morning, with only nature breaking the silence—the sounds of birds singing and the flume cascading joyously down the steep mountainside—our hearts were filled with a deep gratitude for so many things. We were alone among the mountains. The majesty and beauty of those peaks reaching toward the sky brought us peace and joy. We lifted our eyes to the wonder of God's creation and the peace of God filled our hearts.

It was a beautiful trip, and we both agreed that we had done just what we had wanted to do. As we drove back toward our dear home in Longmeadow, Massachusetts, and our dog Gretchen, who was waiting for us, it was hard to decide whether we felt happier going away or coming back. There was so much joy and beauty in both.

Laurel and roses are signs of June. Perhaps laurel is dear to us because the little church in which we were married was decorated with it. Chandeliers, window frames, doorways, and the pulpit, all were draped with fresh pink laurel blossoms and their shiny green leaves, and entwined among them were red roses from Mama's garden. For years and years Bob has given me roses on our anniversary . . . a rose for each year! It is lovely to count your married years in roses. Sometimes he can even pick them from our own garden, for roses are his favorite flower. He grows them, and for him they will bloom and bloom all through the summer and well into the fall.

In June we have to pay attention to our gardens. So much has to be planted in early June, and there is so much scratching, fertilizing, and watering to be done to get things ready for summer. It is fun to set out tiny plants, knowing that in just a little while they will grow into beautiful flowers that can be picked and brought indoors. I love to fill the house with fresh flowers and to enjoy their fragile loveliness. There is not much time for being inside the house except to keep it picked up and orderly, for there is no more enchanting season in which to enjoy the out-of-doors. It seems to give us new strength as we drink in the sunshine and feel our bodies acquiring that characteristic tan of summer which protects us when winter comes. What a gift is sunshine which is ours free of any cost.

My menu for June is a salad—a very special salad which a new friend (I met her when I spoke in Hanover, New Hampshire) had prepared. I had driven from Boston that morning and had arrived early enough to rest a little before friends joined us for a delightful luncheon. This salad tasted so good and was so different that I asked for the recipe, which was sent to me after I had returned home. The beauty of this salad is that it can be served either cold or hot, making it just perfect for either a warm or a cool June day.

ENTREE

Chicken salad		Corn pudding
	Potato chips	
Tomatoes	Swedish cucumbers	Cranberries
	Popovers	
	Strawberry shortcake	
Iced tea		Coffee

CHICKEN SALAD

2½ cups water
1 whole breast of chicken (split)
1 tablespoon lemon juice
1 teaspoon salt
⅛ teaspoon pepper
1 package dry chicken-noodle soup mix

1 cup instant rice
1 cup chopped celery
1 tablespoon chopped onion
1 cup pineapple tidbits
1 teaspoon curry powder
½ teaspoon dry mustard
½ cup mayonnaise
¼ cup sour cream

Cook chicken in the water until tender (20 to 25 minutes). Remove meat in strips, sprinkle with lemon juice, salt, and pepper, and toss; then set aside. Add soup mix and rice to 2 cups of broth in which the chicken was cooked. Cover and bring to a boil; remove from heat and let stand until all the broth is absorbed (15 to 20 minutes). Stir to a fluff. Chop celery, onion, and drained pineapple. Blend curry and mustard into mayonnaise and sour cream. Put all ingredients together, blend thoroughly. Cover and chill thoroughly. Better if made the day before.

To serve hot—increase sour cream to ½ cup, and bake at 350° for 20 minutes.

CORN PUDDING

1 can cream-style corn
1½ cups milk (hot)
2 tablespoons butter
3 eggs (separated)

1 tablespoon cornstarch
2 tablespoons sugar
pinch salt

Beat egg yolks, corn starch, sugar, and salt. Add corn, milk, and butter. Fold in stiffly beaten egg whites. Bake approximately 1½ hours at 350°. Pour into 1½ quart buttered casserole. Set dish in a pan of hot water. Bake approximately 1½ hours at 350°.

For Swedish Cucumbers, refer back to page 23.

POPOVERS

1 package popover mix

Follow the directions, but beat a little longer than indicated. (I beat at least five minutes. You can not overbeat.)

If possible, use an iron or heavy aluminum muffin tin. Preheat the oven to 425° and heat the tins first; then drop a level teaspoon of butter into each cup, turning so that the butter greases the sides. Place the tins in the oven again for 2 minutes, then pour in the batter. Fill a little over half full.

Bake at least 30 minutes without opening the oven door. In all, bake 45 minutes. Remove from the oven and serve piping hot.

I have had better results using a mix than starting from scratch.

STRAWBERRY SHORTCAKE

2 cups biscuit mix
¾ cup medium whipping cream

Mix lightly. Form the dough into a roll and slice it into eight slices. Handle the dough lightly; this is the secret of light biscuits. Bake in 450° oven for 10 to 15 minutes.

Hull and wash 3 pints of strawberries. Slice them into a bowl and cover with a cup of sugar. Let stand for an hour. Stir occasionally.

Whip 1 pint medium cream. Spoon berries over biscuits and top with a generous portion of whipped cream. Garnish each with a whole berry.

GOLD NUGGET:

To remove blood stains, soak article in cold water. Rub in a mild soap and let stand. Rinse in cold water. (Hot water sets blood stains permanently.)

~7

Wondrous Creator, bless our country—our America that gives to us so much to enjoy. Help us to be true to her and to honor and love her with all our hearts. Forbid that we should ever degrade her by word or deed. As we look at that Star-Spangled Banner waving in the blue, remind us that we belong together in good or bad, in peace or war. God grant us peace and brotherhood, and our leaders, wisdom. And may Thy blessing rest over our land. Give us understanding so that we may live each day to the fullest. In gratefulness we pray. Amen.

WHEN July suddenly steps out from the lovely month of June, we are prepared for it. We know that it will be the hottest month of the year, that it will be humid, filled with that sticky heat that sometimes makes the temperature uncomfortable day after day, and even the nights unbearably ovenlike. But in the early morning, when the sky is clear and the sun rises on the eastern horizon, July has its own magic charm. How I love to go out into the garden at that hour and breathe in the beauty of a summer morning. I walk over to the rose beds to admire the dew still on the soft petals and the buds just starting to open. There is something about a rose that is completely unique; it is the touch of the Master's hand, the perfect revelation of His creation, the love of the Father's heart shown in the beauty He so lavishly bestows on earth. I cannot help but marvel at it and sense a oneness with the Eternal as my soul grows increasingly aware of the love of God. My heart offers up a wordless prayer among the roses. I am completely still, but if that prayer could be put into words, it would be the most beautiful one in the world.

Yes, no matter how hot the days are, the mornings are cool and fresh and wonderful. Often I cut some roses for the dining-room table and as I place them, one by one, in the vase, they become precious gifts, dear and lovely, and their fragrance fills the room. All day long they will remind me of my early morning thoughts which were so close to God there in the garden. Roses are a wonderful gift to mankind.

I have a friend in Wisconsin who loves roses, too. Mae is a poet married to a farmer. She has written hundreds of lovely poems and won many prizes for them. There is a oneness between us. We are the kind of friends who do not need to be in constant touch; our thoughts often go to each other. I met Mae at Green Lake, Wisconsin, where we were both vacationing. I think of it as a vacation, although I was actually lecturing and teaching a class in Creative Writing. She was in that class and I found her different from the others. There was a certain mysterious quality about her. As she talked to me, she created a warm, homey feeling; yet at the same time I was conscious that she was reaching out to gather to herself anything new and interesting. She was also deeply spiritual. Mae's faith came first in her life; you did not have to be with her very long before you were conscious of vibrations of peace and joy.

I have visited her big farmhouse several times and met her fine husband and some of her children. The farm kitchen is a beehive of activity, a center where marvelous food is cooked and baked, canned and frozen. The last time I visited Mae she served roast pheasant. It tasted so delicious that I tried not to think of the beautiful live bird. Wild game always takes me a while to enjoy, but this had been prepared especially for me, and it was wonderful.

My friend has many rosebushes in her garden and she gathers the rose petals in the summertime so she can enjoy them even in the cold of winter. Mae has given me her rules for using roses, which I will share with you.

Rose beads are fun to make and very unusual. The story behind them says that strings of beads for counting prayers came to be called rosaries because, in monasteries, the beads were originally made from roses in the following manner.

ROSE BEADS

Grind rose petals very finely in a food grinder for several consecutive days. The old rule was seven times for seven days. But that is hardly necessary. Between grindings keep the petals in an iron skillet or in a container with some iron nails, to darken the pulp. After several days, when the pulp is quite dark and pliable, mold into balls or beads and put them on knitting needles to dry. When dry, string them as desired. Alternating the rose beads with metal or glass beads sets them off nicely.

Or perhaps you would rather preserve rose petals in a jar.

A ROSE JAR

Pick the roses in full bloom, preferably in the morning before the sun gets hot, but after the dew has dried. Do not use the centers, only the petals. Spread them on newspapers or paper toweling to dry. Sprinkle a little salt on them. After several days they will be dry and shrunken. After each batch of petals is dry, put them in a jar, either an ordinary jar or a pot-pourri jar. You may vary what you put with the petals. Ground orris root is one ingredient, as it is a preservative and also adds odor. Ground spices, such as cloves, allspice, or cinnamon, may be included. Some people add fragrant herbs and leaves such as geranium and lavender, some only of eglantine, and a couple of sprays of heliotrope, which blossoms at rose time. In our grandmother's day oils were used. Now they are expensive and not always available, but you can use oil of cloves, oil of lemon, oil of cinnamon, et cetera.

Keep the jar or container well covered except for an hour or two when you want the fragrance to escape into the room.

These rose jars are lovely to have, especially now in our age of automation. The fragrance of the rose petals will calm our busy minds and make the heart of the home happy and secure with the memories that flood the soul.

But there are also things to eat which can be made from roses. There is a delicate jelly and rose-hip soup which

82

my Mama always made. It was one of Papa's favorite sweets.

ROSE-HIP JELLY

Here is a rich natural source of vitamin C right on your doorstep.

Rose hips (either wild or cultivated roses)
Water
Apple juice
Pectin
Sugar

Wash rose hips in cold water after removing the stems. Add two cups water to each cup of rose hips and boil for 15 minutes. Mash the hips with a potato masher, and simmer for 10 more minutes. Set the mixture aside for 24 hours in a glass or stainless-steel container. Then strain the juice through a cloth bag; squeeze the bag lightly, but do not squeeze it dry as this will make the jelly cloudy. To one or two cups juice, add one cup apple juice and one box pectin. Bring this mixture to a good rolling boil, then add 4½ cups sugar, stirring occasionally. Boil for 6 or 7 minutes or until the jelly drops from a spoon in thickened sheets. Remove from heat, skim, and pour into sterilized jelly glasses. Cover with melted paraffin.

After the paraffin sets, cap, label and store in a cool place.

ROSE-HIP SOUP (*Nypon-Soppa*)

3 cups fresh or 2 cups dry rose hips
3 pints water
¾ cup sugar
　 salt
1½ tablespoons potato flour
¼ cup shredded almonds

Place the rose hips, which have been thoroughly cleaned, in boiling water. Cover and cook until tender; then strain, forcing the hips through a sieve. Take 4½ cups liquid from this process (add cold water if needed to make full amount). Return to kettle, add sugar and a dash of salt and stir in potato flour which has been mixed with a little water to make a smooth paste. Bring to a boil, stirring constantly. Pour into soup tureen and add almonds. Chill soup.

Top with whipped cream and serve with rusks.

Dry rose hips or packaged ready-to-heat *Nypon-soppa* can be bought in any Scandinavian food store.

QUICK RUSKS

1 cup butter	1 teaspoon ground carda-
1½ cups sugar	mom seed
2 eggs	4½ cups flour
½ teaspoon salt	1 cup milk
3 teaspoons baking powder	

Cream the butter and add sugar and unbeaten eggs. Mix in salt and baking powder, cardamom and flour together; add to first mixture, alternating with milk. Stir well. Place mixture in well-greased 13x9 pan. Sprinkle a little sugar on top. Bake at 350° for 30 to 35 minutes.

Remove from oven and cut into narrow strips—4 across and 18 or 20 down. Place pieces on a cookie sheet and return to the oven. Bake 45 minutes longer at 250°. Turn pieces and brown 15 minutes longer.

The rusks will be hard and crisp and should be crumbled into the *Nypon-soppa*, as crackers would be crumbled in hot soup. Extras can be stored in tight containers and used as a snack with milk or coffee.

In July we certainly don't want to think about cleaning house, but there is one place that I always save to tidy up during this month, and that is the cellar. On a hot day it is cool in the basement and I think it is fun to clean it at this time. Because the cellar is part of the home, it cannot be neglected if we are to have an orderly household. I always seem to acquire a lot of pep when I start setting things in order down there. Somehow during the year many things accumulate. There are boxes to go through where you may find all sorts of interesting things—old letters, pamphlets, clippings, and other mementos. If you are like me, you hate to part with things that are dear to you. That is why I keep a big box on which is printed in large letters, "The Throw-Away Box." Into that box goes everything I ought to throw away, but can't quite make myself give up just yet. After the cellar is clean, I go through all these things again—some really do get thrown out, others are kept a little while longer. But during the following months most of them disappear.

Walls, ceilings, and floors in the cellar need to be swept and washed, and all clothing stored there needs to be aired in the sunshine to avoid a musty smell in the house. A cellar can be an interesting place to spend time on a hot summer day. All we need is to make up our minds to do the job and put our hearts and souls into it.

It is smart to mark the contents of each box stored in the cellar; it saves a lot of time when you are looking for a particular item. But it is also a good policy not to keep too many things you don't need, especially old letters and cards. Mama always said that when one reaches sixty years of age, it is time to start "clearing the deck." Everything of sentimental value to you alone should be disposed of. It saves loved ones a lot of work after a person has died. Some things can be given to the Good Will or the Salvation Army at this time. Certain items meant for family members and loved ones should be marked and a cheerful little note enclosed. To do all this lifts a burden from many hearts. It is a great thing to accomplish in a lifetime, for after sixty one should travel light. How relieved our family was after Mama had died that there was not a thing to clear out of her house except the necessary household items. Mama had prepared wisely. She had packed away her belongings as she knew that one day she would take a trip from which there would be no return. She handled all this with such sense, foresight, and dignity that it set a pattern which I would like to follow.

Perhaps we could also call July the Friendship Month. Many people travel in this month. And as we travel, we meet wonderful new people, some of whom become lifelong friends. It widens our minds to talk to new people and share their experiences. They give to us a special gift and we gain tolerance and understanding as we relax and share stories from our lives. It makes life interesting. And new friends are a real treasure to add to the old faithful ones who have been with us through the years. So when we travel, let us give our friendship unstintingly and it will be returned to us in double measure.

And we cannot live through this month without feeling the magnificent power of Independence Day—July Fourth. It will always remain a great day and will draw us closer to our wonderful land if we think of its meaning. Ours is a blessed land! It is a beautiful land! It is a good land! And we should plant these thoughts in the mind of the younger generation as soon as they can understand. The love of country should come next to the love of God in a nation. We should never degrade our own land. We should never think the wrong way about it. Whatever the world says about us, we are a good nation and we have given to the world more than any other nation. In wartime, giving our men and materials, raised our taxes and deprived us of certain things. We did this to help others. We did not fight to confiscate land; we fought to help and to save the world from disaster. America has always extended a helping hand to those suffering from hunger or tragedy. So let us hold our country high and stand back of our leaders, praying that they may be wise and led by God in all they do. A very wise President, who at a much too early age gave his life for his country, said: "Ask not what your country can do for you—ask what you can do for your country." How right he was, for he knew that in giving we would be receiving and that this partnership would bind us to each other in righteous living and brotherhood.

The Fourth of July has changed a lot since our family first came to this country. How noisy it was the week before the big day—and especially the night before. No one could sleep. There were explosions of many firecrackers— each bang louder than the one before. But that time is past. Too many unfortunate mishaps made the states enact laws forbidding that kind of celebration. But we still have beautiful public displays of fireworks in most of our cities and towns—the one thing left from the time when fireworks were the climax of a happy Fourth of July.

I have a fine Fourth of July story related to me by my friend Mae, who shared it with me one lovely fall day when I was lecturing in Wisconsin and had stopped in for a visit. We had taken a long walk in the sunshine and it felt just like summer, although it was late September. Later we got into the old car and drove past the fields. What fun it was for me to see the cows, chickens, and pigs, and to breathe in that fresh country air. Suddenly Mae stopped the car.

"Let's sit down on that old hayrake," she suggested.

We walked to it along a narrow path with the woods on one side of us and the fields on the other.

"If we sit here real quiet for a while," said Mae, "perhaps we'll see a fox."

I arose in alarm. "Aren't foxes dangerous?" I asked.

"No, they're scared to death of people. They wouldn't come near if they saw us. They'd be more frightened than you are."

"Oh, I'm not that scared," I laughed. "I was just startled. I had no idea there were wild animals so near the farm."

"There are wild ones all right," said Mae. "Ever so often we lose a batch of chickens when the foxes decide to have a party."

"I wish I could see one—a real, live fox. It would be interesting."

"It doesn't happen very often," said Mae, "but last Fourth of July I saw some. Do you want to hear a true fox story?"

"Please. I'm all ears."

Mae was quiet for a moment, as if she were taking herself back to the previous summer, and then she began her story:

"It was early morning on Independence Day and it had been a busy week on the farm. Somehow I was just fed up with everything. I put a large casserole of beans in the oven to bake. It was the last of the food to get ready for the big family picnic that afternoon. The weather that day was perfect. My youngest daughter was busy with the dishes. Suddenly I made a decision.

"'I'm going bird watching for a while, dear,' I said. 'Keep an eye on the beans.'"

"'Good for you, Mae,' said my husband, who had just appeared at the kitchen door. 'I'm glad you're getting away by yourself for a while. Hop in the truck. I'm just about to go down to the meadows. I'll take you down to all the beautiful birds.'

"We drove down over the fields and suddenly it was good to think of resting. A farm certainly has a way of draining your strength.

"He left me here and told me he'd be back for me in an hour, so I took up residence on the hayrake. The sun felt so good and the sky was so blue. It was wonderful to have this quiet place to come to and I was grateful for our big farm as I sat there relaxing, feeling how very tired my body was. The birds were slow in showing up. Well, birds or no birds, I thought, this is a good place to rest. And then—what do you suppose?—instead of a beautiful bird there came slinking down the path, as big as life, Papa Fox himself. He was out for a morning hunt,

I guessed, down in the marsh. His arrival was totally un-expected and he did not see me, so I was able to watch him closely as he picked his way until he disappeared into the tall marsh grass. This was worth every moment of the day, seeing that handsome fox and I kept watching in the same direction. Just a few minutes later, to my surprise, Mama Fox appeared, dragging herself out of the marsh grass from the exact spot where Papa Fox had disappeared. Her coat was wet and unkempt.

"Impossible, I thought to myself. My husband would never believe this. Just wait until I tell him. These could be the same foxes that ate the pheasants that he loved to hunt.

"I had brought a magazine with me and I thumbed through the pages, but I was too excited to read. I still had almost an hour in which to relax, but now I was full of pep. This had been such fun. Then I heard a strange noise to my left, and I turned to look. I had to rub my eyes. It just couldn't happen. But it had; I was seeing it with my own eyes. It was the baby—the cutest little fox I had ever laid my eyes on. He came running down the path full tilt, his bright eyes not missing a thing. He almost ran into me on the hayrake, then suddenly he saw me. His eyes took on that I'd-better-get-out-of-here-in-a-hurry look and he was off in a flash. I stayed there spellbound for a few minutes. My heart was beating in wild excitement. Then I left the hayrake and started to walk through the hay field which had just come alive with a second crop of alfalfa. Conscious that I was still tired, I stretched out full length on the soft, sun-warmed ground and closed my eyes in perfect relaxation. A little noise reached my ear. I sat up quickly and sure enough, the world was full of foxes. This one was half-grown, and he would have run right into my lap if I had not sat up. Frankly this was enough. I'd had it! Four foxes in one short hour! I picked up my belongings and started toward home and there just around the corner came my husband in the old truck. I had hardly time to climb in before I began.

" 'I'm going to tell you something you won't believe . . .'

"Of course he listened, but he never said a word, just stepped on the gas pedal, went home, and loaded his gun."

The story ended and so did the spell.

"Oh, Mae," I cried, "he didn't—he didn't go down there and shoot that lovely fox family."

Mae laughed at my anxiety.

"Of course not," she answered calmly. "He never even saw their shadows. Haven't you ever heard the saying, 'smart as a fox'?"

"Oh, I'm relieved," I exclaimed happily. "If he had shot even one of them, the whole story would be spoiled. I was just thinking that perhaps they were having a fox picnic that day."

And that was the story of a farm wife who went bird watching and saw only foxes.

The fox story made me think of all the families of wild creatures in the forests and wildernesses of our big country. We so seldom get a glimpse of them as they run free in their own world. There is so much we haven't seen and should see in our America, from Alaska to Hawaii, from

Maine to California. What a land we live in and what beauty and scenery there is for us to enjoy!

And now our menu for the hottest month of the year:

ENTREE

Cold meat platter with stuffed tomatoes
De luxe creamed potatoes   Fresh garden peas
Radishes
Quicky blueberry muffins
Iced coffee   Iced tea

DESSERT

Strawberry-rhubarb pie

Arrange a variety of cold sliced meat on a platter and garnish with radishes and stuffed tomatoes.

STUFFED TOMATOES

Scoop out the tomatoes so they are hollow. Mix the pulp of each tomato with one level teaspoon mayonnaise and one teaspoon tiny cubes of cucumber. Fill the hollow tomatoes with this mixture and top with a sprig of parsley.

DE LUXE CREAMED POTATOES

⅓ stick of margarine or butter

1½ tablespoons flour

1 cup milk

2 tablespoons chopped parsley

4 thin slices white American cheese cut in tiny cubes

3 or 4 large potatoes—cooked and cubed

salt and Accent to taste

Melt margarine and stir in flour. Use low heat and watch carefully so it does not brown. Add milk and stir. When the mixture has come to a boil and thickened, add parsley and cheese and stir again. Add potatoes and mix lightly as the mixture heats through. (Don't stir hard or the potatoes will lose their shape.) Flavor with salt and Accent to taste.

FRESH GARDEN PEAS

Shell peas and place in lightly salted water. Boil uncovered until peas are tender, 10 to 15 minutes. Drain and flavor with butter, salt, and Accent to taste.

QUICKY BLUEBERRY MUFFINS

⅔ stick butter	1 teaspoon baking powder
½ cup confectioner's sugar	½ cup milk
1 egg	1 tablespoon regular flour
1 cup self-rising flour	1 cup blueberries

Cream butter and sugar until light and fluffy. Add egg and stir thoroughly. Add self-rising flour with baking powder mixed in, alternating with milk. Toss blueberries with regular flour and add to mixture.

Pour mixture into well-greased muffin tins. Fill tins ⅔ full. Bake in 375° oven about 20 minutes or until brown.

STRAWBERRY-RHUBARB PIE

Pie Shell

2 cups flour	not over 2 tablespoons
1 teaspoon salt	water
¾ cup vegetable shortening	

Pour the flour into a bowl and mix in salt and shortening. Work with finger tips until the flour has absorbed the shortening. Then pour a tiny bit of water on the dough and blend lightly into the mixture. Pick up the tiny lumps and put into another bowl. Press the tiny lumps between your hands to make a big ball. Give it one good, hard squeeze, then cut in half.

Flour the baking board and rolling pin. Roll out one crust

and fit it into pie plate. Put in filling and wet sides of pie shell with water. Roll out the other crust, put it on top and press down the sides to seal. Flute the sides and prick the top with a fork a few times for air holes.

FILLING

1 cup rhubarb (cubed)
1 cup strawberries
1 cup water
1 cup sugar (and ½ cup extra if needed)

3 tablespoons cornstarch blended in a little cold water into a smooth paste
a dash salt

Put rhubarb and strawberries together into a pan and cook about 10 minutes in one cup water. Add one cup sugar first and taste. If it is too tart, add the other half cup. Add salt. Bring to a rapid boil and pour in the cornstarch mixture. Stir slowly. When thick, remove from pan and let stand until cool. Pour into pie shell and bake at 350° for 35 minutes. Cool and serve.

GOLD NUGGET:

Read Psalm 104 together as a family. Memorize parts of it and you will have gained special food for the soul.

❦8

Thank you, dear God, that we can worship
you from any place and that you have given
us so many things to enjoy in the summertime.
We pray for special protection as we drive,
and most of all that our eyes may open wide
to see You in everything beautiful. We pray
for those who are ill and poor and cannot take
a trip nor travel. Make us willing to share
what we have with others. Bless all who worship in churches today and those who preach
your gospel. As a family, our hearts overflow
with gratitude and joy for all we have been
given by the Father of mankind. Amen.

WHAT I remember most vividly about the
month of August in my native land is the moonlight. It
seemed to be the most beautiful moonlight of the year. I
can still see that great big yellow moon rising slowly from
behind the mountain, changing from gold to silver as it

rose, transforming the whole world into an enchanted fairyland. Oftentimes we went out in a rowboat on the lake below our home on such nights. As we glided along on the still water, only our oars dipping up and down broke the perfect reflection of the moon. People had told me about the magic of moonbeams. They said that if you could engulf yourself in the moon's light and could reach out and catch a beam, holding it just for a second, you could make any wish you wanted to and it would come true. I never stopped to reason that one could not catch a moonbeam, so I was forever trying to get under that magic spell. Alas, I never succeeded.

Late August was also lingonberry time. It was then that we would go every day to pick those little bright red berries until Mama said we had enough. They grew everywhere in the deep forest on tiny, low, green plants. They grew in clumps and when they were abundant, it was easy to fill a pail. Mama cooked them in a big kettle and added the proper amount of sugar. Then each batch was poured into a barrel kept in the earth cellar where it stood side by side with other barrels containing salt herring, dill pickles, and salt pork; there, too, were the crock with preserved eggs and the bin filled to the brim with potatoes. When all those barrels, crocks, and bins were filled to the top, we were ready for the long winter months.

Papa used to take us children, usually two at a time, to pick lingonberries with him. Sometimes we went the night before, walking for miles and sleeping overnight in a hayloft in some farmer's barn. I can still feel a chill up my spine when I remember how spooky it was in the semidarkness trying to find the right place to lie down. The hay pricked if you turned a certain way. There was no place to undress or wash, so we slept with our clothes on and washing had to wait until we got home again. In the morning we would awaken at the first glimpse of dawn, stand up, and shake the stiffness out of our bodies before we scrambled off toward the woodland with our pails.

What memories we have of such mornings, when we sat on a tree stump to have breakfast, which Mama had so thoughtfully put in a big bag for each of us. Nothing ever tasted better. Then the picking would begin. After a few hours we grew a little weary and our backs ached, but we knew we'd better hurry if we wanted to start home early, for Papa would never leave until all the pails were full.

Once I wandered off a bit too far from Papa and my brother. I saw so many berries that I just reached out for them. They seemed larger farther away, so I kept going until I noticed suddenly how quiet it was around me. I didn't hear the voices of the others, only the chirping of the birds. I called to Papa as loudly as I could, but there was no answer. It was a big forest, and I was hopelessly lost. I walked and walked, but I had no idea how I could get back to the place from which I had started. Finally, I sat down on the roots of a tree, leaned against the trunk and the tears began to come. I was so frightened and so alone. Directly in front of me was a big cave with a dark opening in the rustic stone structure. I was too tired to walk any farther; perhaps if I sat there Papa would find me when he realized that I was missing. . . .

I don't know how long I had been sitting there when I

heard a strange noise from inside the cave. It sounded as if heavy feet were walking. There was a shuffling and a dragging noise, and then I could even hear a heavy breathing. Whatever it was, it was coming nearer and nearer. I wanted to get up and run, but my feet refused to move. All I could do was to sit there and stare at the opening . . . and wonder . . . and wait. Then I saw him! He was a big, big man—oh, so much taller than Papa—and he had the ugliest face I had ever seen and a long beard covering his chin. His nostrils trembled as he appeared at the entrance of the cave and his large fish eyes stared my way. I tried to make myself very small, but I could not escape his look. When he discovered me, he laughed—an awful, gleeful laugh that roared like thunder.

"What have we here?" he said. "It looks like a little girl who's lost."

I tried to be brave, realizing he must be a giant—a real one—just like the ones I had read about in fairy tales.

"That is just what I am—lost!" I said in a very loud voice.

He laughed again, not quite so loudly. "That is what I like to have for supper. Nothing tastes better than lost little girls."

My heart began to beat so hard I was afraid he would hear how frightened I was. "I am not the kind that you eat," I heard myself tell him.

"Oh, I'm not fussy. I eat all kinds."

"But I know I wouldn't taste very good," I insisted. "Please, sir, can't I work for you instead?"

He glared at me. "What can you do?" he demanded.

"I can cook and wash dishes and mend socks——"

"And can you dance and sing?" he asked in a slightly friendlier tone.

"No. I'm not too good at those things because I've only learned to work real well."

"Well," said the giant nonchalantly, "we can always catch frogs for supper. Are you a good frog catcher?"

"Sure! I catch them with my bare hands."

He snorted. "What else would you use?"

"Oh, some people catch them on a fish hook."

"You *are* a funny one! Perhaps I'll keep you."

"Thank you, sir. I'll work very, very hard." But even as those words were being spoken, I was trying to think of a way to escape while he was asleep.

"Come," he barked and took my hand in his hairy one. "We'd better go into the cave so you can begin to work."

Then suddenly I knew that I would never, never go with him into that deep, dark cave. I would never work for him as his servant. I would go home to my own Mama and Papa. I snatched my hand away and began to run. I ran faster and faster, but I could hear him running after me, uttering awful threats of what he would do with me when he caught me. Just as I thought I was getting away, I stumbled and fell. Then I knew I was doomed. . . .

At that very moment I heard my Papa's voice. It seemed to come from far away:

"Look! There she is, the little thing. She's curled up in a ball by that tree root. She looks as if she's been crying. Let's wake her up!"

I opened my eyes wide and looked up at Papa, who was smiling at me. I reached out my arms. "Oh, Papa, he's gone. You scared him away. Now he can't take me."

"Who is gone?" asked Papa.

"The giant, of course, the one who was going to eat me."

I was trembling and Papa held me close; never had anything felt so wonderful as to be back with my own Papa.

"There was no giant, dear," he comforted. "You just had a very bad dream."

I didn't argue; I just snuggled closer to Papa. If it was a dream, it certainly had me plenty scared and I would be very happy if there were no giant. But I wasn't too sure that Papa was right.

It took me years to forget that day. Even now, at times, I can close my eyes and see it all again so clearly. And the next time we went berrypicking, I never strayed more than a few feet from Papa. The deep forest did not seem friendly to me any more. I knew that in the shadows of its big trees there were caves and never again in my life would I sit alone near one of them. Childhood has long passed now, but that dream has never faded, even with the years. There is something very mysterious about some dreams; they seem to stay vividly alive even when you have become a grandmother.

August is the last month of the summer. September often has a bit of summer in it, but the spell disappears with August. Perhaps that is why it is so important to make the most of this month, even if its days are hot and humid. August nights, however, as a rule, are quite pleasant.

This month is especially good for family picnics. Picnics

and summer belong together. Children will always remember the big basket loaded with food, the gallon jug
of ice-cold lemonade, and the thermos of coffee. Bathing
suits and bath towels were packed in the family automobile as we took off for the mountains or the seashore or a
small lake near home.

Sometimes we never got any farther than our very own
park. But it was always a pretty spot where we unpacked
our basket, cleaned off the picnic table, and began to
pile up the things which came from our basket. And food
tasted more scrumptious than ever when eaten outside.

Here is a menu that we often used for a picnic day.
But if you aren't picnic-minded, you can always use it for
an August day at home. Sometimes picnic food tastes just
as good in the backyard or on the porch.

NOON MEAL

Fried chicken
Potato salad with chives

| Tomatoes | Cucumbers | Celery sticks |
| Olives | Dill-pickle sticks | |

Fresh rye bread
Apple pie with cheese

| Lemonade | Watermelon | Coffee |

MIDAFTERNOON SNACK

| Cinnamon buns | Oatmeal cookies |
| Milk | Coffee |

SUPPER

Sandwiches
Fresh fruit

| Lemonade | Coffee |

FRIED CHICKEN

2 tablespoons instant chicken broth powder
1 cup flour
1 cup breadcrumbs
1 teaspoon paprika
Enough chicken to allow one-half chicken per person
2 sticks margarine

2 tablespoons grated lemon peel
1 teaspoon Accent (no salt)
¼ cup cooking sherry
2 or 3 tablespoons heavy cream

Crush the instant chicken broth with a rolling pin until it is as fine as meal. In a bowl mix all the dry ingredients together.

Wash the chicken parts. Put some of the dry mixture in a heavy paper bag. Drop the chicken pieces in one at a time and shake until well coated.

Melt 1 stick of margarine in a frying pan and let brown. Fry the chicken parts until golden brown on both sides. Do not salt—there is enough salt in the margarine. Melt 1 stick of margarine in a baking pan. When the chicken is golden brown, remove from the frying pan and place in the baking pan. Bake in a 300° oven for about 1 hour, baste with the melted margarine every 10 minutes. After it has baked for 30 minutes, sprinkle cream and sherry alternately over the chicken and baste again.

POTATO SALAD WITH CHIVES

7 medium-sized potatoes (boiled and peeled)
¼ cup melted butter
1 teaspoon white vinegar
½ cup finely cut celery
1 tablespoon chopped parsley
2 tablespoons chopped chives

4 slices Bermuda onion pulled apart
1 teaspoon salt
½ cup mayonnaise
2 hard-boiled eggs, chopped (optional)

Cut the potatoes into small cubes. Mix the melted butter and vinegar and sprinkle over the potatoes. Add celery, parsley, chives, and onions. Sprinkle on salt. Add mayonnaise. Mix lightly. Add eggs, if desired.

For a picnic, pack in a glass or porcelain container and keep cool, or pack in ice if you are traveling.

Prepare celery sticks and cucumber slices and place them in separate plastic bags. Leave tomatoes whole and slice just before serving. Leave olives and dill pickles in their jars.

The recipe for fresh rye bread is found on page 10.

Fix lemonade and put in a gallon jug with plenty of ice. Fill thermos with hot coffee. Bring sugar and cream separately.

Put a whole watermelon in the picnic basket and be sure to bring a good sharp knife.

APPLE PIE

5 or 6 apples	½ teaspoon cloves
1 cup sugar	1 tablespoon flour
1 teaspoon cinnamon	butter
½ teaspoon nutmeg	

Peel the apples and slice thin. Place in a bowl and mix in sugar, cinnamon, nutmeg, cloves, and flour. Toss lightly. Arrange in a pie shell (prepared according to recipe on page 93) and top with dabs of butter.

Bake in a 425° oven for 40 minutes.

Wrap the pie in foil and wrap the cubes of cheese separately.

CINNAMON BUNS

Use the basic coffee-bread dough recipe on page 35.

Roll the dough on a baking board as you would cookie dough. Spread with ½ cup soft butter and sprinkle with sugar and cinnamon. Roll the dough into a long roll and cut slices 1¼ inches thick with a sharp knife. Place on a greased baking sheet. Make indentations in the buns in two places, using your index finger and thumb. Let dough rise to double size. Brush each bun with melted butter and sprinkle with sugar. Bake in a 375° oven for 15 to 20 minutes.

MAMA'S OATMEAL COOKIES

1 cup butter	1 teaspoon salt
2 cups sugar	2 cups flour
2 eggs beaten	2 cups oatmeal
1 teaspoon baking soda dissolved in 2 tablespoons water	1 cup raisins

Cream butter and sugar until light and fluffy. Add eggs and stir again. Add baking soda and salt, which have been sifted with the flour (except 2 tablespoonfuls) and oatmeal. Coat the raisins with 2 tablespoons of flour before adding them to the mixture. Mix all ingredients thoroughly and then drop by the spoonful onto a greased baking sheet.

Bake in a 425° oven for 10 to 15 minutes or until golden brown.

For picnic sandwiches I suggest cheese and tunafish. Be sure they are well wrapped in wax paper and kept in a cool container until suppertime. If they cannot be kept cool, choose something other than tunafish, something like peanut butter that does not spoil easily.

Peaches, pears, apples, grapes, and cherries make a colorful and appetizing end to a picnic.

Long ago when our girls were small, Rocky Neck, Connecticut, was our favorite picnic spot. How we loved to seek out a nice hillside and set up our table. Then we rushed to take a swim to cool off. The memories are still aglow as I write this. We stayed all day long, usually on a Sunday, since this was our only entirely free day. I always minded missing church in the morning and because of this we held our own service in the automobile while we were driving. One of the girls would read the Scripture and we would discuss the passage as our sermon. And although Bob's eyes could not close during prayer, we did repeat the Lord's Prayer together, and as we rode along, we had the feeling that we had worshiped in a delightful way in spite of our absence from church. We often sang hymns, too; that we could all do together. Strangely enough, after that service on wheels, my heart was light, and I felt it was good for us to go to the beach as a family, even on a Sunday.

Oh, the wonder of summertime! The beauty of it! The joy it brings and the contentment! In August I feel that every housewife should have a party of her own. There are so many women friends she seldom sees. Why not have a garden party some afternoon when the garden is at its best?

It is fun to get ready for this kind of party. It should not be too big—about eight. It might be called a do-nothing party, for it is good to get together just to sit in the garden, just to relax and talk. The conversation is never at a lull; there are so many things to discuss—children, the family, vacations, and plans. Everyone is a contributor. Refreshments should be simple but with a festive touch, and they must be prepared beforehand so the hostess can be with her guests most of the time. If the garden has an umbrella table, that would be a perfect spot; if not, set up a card table with a gay cloth and a centerpiece

of garden flowers. Have some colorful napkins, too. I
found some flower-printed ones which say, "I am glad
you came." People love those napkins and I have had
many compliments on them. You can always be on the
lookout for these things which add to the pleasure of a
get-together. Cups, silver, and plates should be ready on
a big tray; nothing can be set out too far ahead of serving
time because of those little insects that always come unin-
vited when people eat out of doors. But everything can
be ready to take outside a few minutes before the guests
arrive. It is a good idea to eat when the guests come; then
the free time afterwards can be enjoyed by all. Let us
say party time is three o'clock in the afternoon. We will
serve:

Frozen party salad

Vinerbröd   Cup cakes

Mints   Hot coffee   Salted nuts

FROZEN SALAD

1 teaspoon gelatine

3 tablespoons pineapple syrup

⅔ cup heavy cream

⅓ cup mayonnaise

1 teaspoon powdered sugar

1 tablespoon maraschino
syrup

2 tablespoons lemon juice

1 banana cut fine

¾ cup diced pineapple

½ cup maraschino cherries
cut fine

Soak the gelatine in pineapple syrup and dissolve over hot
water.

Whip the cream until stiff. Gradually beat in the mayonnaise. Add gelatine and the rest of the ingredients.

Place in a large freezer tray and freeze for 4 to 5 hours,

stirring occasionally. Cut into squares and serve on bib-lettuce leaves; garnish with a rose-petal-cut cherry and a few nuts.

VINERBRÖD

3 cups flour	¾ cup milk
1 egg	½ pound butter (soft)
⅓ cup sugar	1 egg white
2 packages yeast dissolved in ¼ cup lukewarm milk	extra sugar

Place the flour in a bowl and make a groove in the middle of it. Into this groove drop egg; add sugar, yeast, and milk. Stir until the mixture becomes dough. Roll out on a well-floured baking board. When it is manageable, flour the top lightly and spread on all the butter. Fold in three folds and roll out again. Repeat this rolling and folding three or four times. When it has been folded for the last time, cut long, thin slices of dough and twist them into a pretzel shape. Brush with stiffly beaten egg white, and dip in sugar. Place on a greased baking sheet and let rise until they are double in size.

Bake in a 425° oven for 15 minutes or until golden brown. Remove from the oven and let cool. Then serve. They taste best right after they are baked.

CUPCAKES

Make cupcakes from your favorite cake recipe in tiny cupcake tins. After they are baked and cooled, frost as follows.

FROSTING IN THREE PARTS

First:
  2 tablespoons cream
  ½ cup butter
  confectioner's sugar (enough for spreading consistently)
  2 tablespoons orange juice
  2 tablespoons lemon juice

Cream butter with cream and sugar; add juice and stir until fluffy. Add only as much sugar as you need to achieve spreading consistency.

Second:
Divide the frosting into three parts, placing each in a different bowl.

Third:
To the first mixture add a few drops of red food coloring and stir.
To the second mixture add a few drops of green food coloring and stir.
To the third mixture add chopped pineapple but no coloring.
Frost cupcakes and arrange on a tray, alternating the colors.

What could be nicer than a beautiful afternoon in the garden, a charming hostess, and happy guests?

The summer is slowly fading away. August gives us so many different fruits and vegetables, and nowadays, instead of canning, we can freeze them and put them away for the winter. I can recall how, years ago, we housewives used to can and preserve. I shall always remember the fruit closet we had in the cellar. How I loved to fill the shelves and how hard I worked making tomato juice, putting up all sorts of vegetables, and labeling them. There they stood—shelf after shelf of jars and glasses of vegetables, fruits, and jellies. When it was all done, how rich I felt and how well my family was provided with food. Winter could come with its snow and ice, but we had a little bit of summer tucked away in that closet in the cellar.

I shall never get the satisfaction from freezing things that I did from the hard work of canning. But no matter how it is done, wise is the housewife who takes the time and makes the effort to think ahead and prepare for the unknown.

GOLD NUGGET:
  A gentle tone of voice on a hot, humid August day and a smile to accompany it are as refreshing to a weary person as a cool breeze when day is done.

❧9

So exceptionally tender
Is this month called September
As summer is fading away.
When it sadly surrenders,
No power can hold it to stay.
For fall in its boldness,
Its cruelness and coldness,
Will conquer; there is no delay.
 It nips
 And scars.
 It strips
 And bares.
And darkness will shorten the day.

Our prayer in September
Is, Lord, make us tender
As year after year fades away.
Let kindness and love
Fill our hearts from above
That from goodness we never will stray.

It is like a dream, I say to myself, that this
summer is almost over. The joys that it brought will soon

be but a memory, and when September has completed a little over half its days, it is fall. Here in New England then, as well as in many parts of our great country, we shall soon feel cold winds and Jack Frost will be nipping the late flowers in our gardens. How we hope that fall will be beautiful, with lots of sunshine; that it lingers a long while before winter sets in and the days grow short and dark.

Perhaps that is why we so cherish the last few summer days and look with delight at our flowers, knowing that we can still pick armloads of them to bring into the house. Now, too, there are so many good things to eat, fresh from fruit trees and vines—apples, peaches, pears, grapes, and many others. How fortunate we are to have so much to be grateful for in this split month that both summer and fall claim.

In September children all across our nation go back to school and mothers have more time for their homes. For the first time in a long spell the housewife might have a few minutes to sit down and think and evaluate life. The days speed by so quickly and there is so much activity that thinking has become a rare luxury.

Some people might feel that we don't need to think any more; there are computers that will do it for us. These mechanical devices do almost everything; just name it, and there is a machine for it. But no matter how wonderful those computers are, I still like to do my own thinking. My brain needs the exercise of wrestling with problems and considering in depth the happenings of our world— and I need the stillness that accompanies meditation.

The younger generation has a totally different outlook on life though. The other day I asked the boy who helps us in the garden about this very thing.

"Donald," I said, "how can the young people of today think with all the noise that always surrounds them?"

He looked at me for a moment as if he were digging deep down within himself for the answer. Then he gave me a big grin. "Mrs. Bjorn," he said, "the youth of today prefers not to think; so we don't."

I went back to the house and settled in a lounge chair on the porch, and Donald went back to his weeding after turning up the transistor radio he always carries and places beside him in the grass. I was a bit perplexed. What a strange new generation, I thought, and they will be the leaders in tomorrow's world.

What a different world it was from the one in which I was young, and how values have changed. My mind wandered back to that long ago, and I wondered at how much time we had had for leisure and thinking. "Was our work harder?" I questioned myself. And I knew it was. "Was there more of it?" Yes, I knew that to be the case. "Then why did we still have so much leisure?" Then I remembered the ways in which we took time.

I remembered with delight the coffee hour at four o'clock every afternoon. Every Swedish home observed this coffee hour; they always made time for it. Usually company gathered with us around the table. It was almost a ritual, as I think of it now. Coffee was always served in the best room in the house and the good coffee cups were used. Mama tied a crisp embroidered apron over her skirt and saw that her hair was neatly brushed.

How well I can remember that often, about three thirty in the afternoon, Mama would say to me, "Run over to Fru Almgren's, like a good girl, and ask if she will drop in to have afternoon coffee with us."

And away I would go, as fast as my legs could carry me. It was fun to knock on the Almgrens' door to extend such a pleasant invitation.

At the same time Mama might send one of the other children to Fru Karlsson's with the same message. And if Papa happened to have a caller, he, too, would be invited to join us.

The coffee hour might have had a formal setting, but no matter how much dignity there was in that room, it did not shut out the fun and laughter. Mama poured the steaming brown coffee from the shiny copper coffeepot and after grace had been said, the conversation got into full swing. Little details of home life were shared by neighbors and friends and even the most trivial incidents seemed interesting.

"Let me tell you what happened to my new red wool sweater," Mrs. Almgren would say. "My Lisa, who has reached the age of ten and is always playing grownup, wanted to show me that she could do the washing all by herself. My beautiful sweater was her victim. She poured boiling water over it, and now, let me tell you, it is the size of a large mitten."

We all laughed, although it was really not a laughing matter. But the tone of Mrs. Almgren's voice and the smile on her face made us see the amusing side. She had contributed the story for our enjoyment, and it would lead to another incident from someone else around the table.

113

Sharing the small, everyday happenings created a feeling of warmth and togetherness.

The afternoon coffee was not an elaborate event. Mama usually served coffee bread and *skorpor*, which she always had on hand. But occasionally she would delight us with one of her special *Socker-Kakas* and that made us all feel as if this were a special occasion. The *skorpor* were crisp and brown and we always dunked them in our coffee. Somehow they always seemed to take the prize; nothing else tasted quite as good. These *skorpor* were different from the ones we eat with the *Nypon-soppa*, since these were made from yeast dough. And if you are tempted to have an old-fashioned coffee party, here are the recipes for *skorpor* and *socker-kaka*.

FOUR O'CLOCK *SKORPOR*

Use the basic coffee-bread dough recipe on page 35.

Roll the dough into long loaves and place on a baking sheet. Let rise to double size and bake in a 350° oven for about 45 minutes to 1 hour. Remove from oven and cool.

When the bread is cold, slice with a sharp knife into pieces 1½ inches thick. Then cut the slices lengthwise in two or three pieces. Place them on a baking sheet, and dry in a 400° oven for five minutes (until brown). Then reduce the oven temperature to 200° and let them dry for an additional 55 minutes.

Store in a tightly covered container in a cool place.

MAMA'S *SOCKER-KAKA*

    2 eggs
    pinch of salt
    1 cup sugar
    1 cup cake-flour (sifted)

114

1½ teaspoons baking powder
½ cup hot milk
    a piece of butter the size of a walnut
1 teaspoon grated lemon rind.

Beat eggs with electric beater until light. Add the salt and sugar and beat for about ten minutes. Carefully fold in flour in which the baking powder has been mixed. Gradually stir in the hot milk in which the butter has been melted. Add lemon rind. Stir lightly until smooth.

Pour into a small tube pan which has been carefully greased with butter and dusted with breadcrumbs. (A square baking pan can be used.)

Bake in 325° oven for 30 minutes. Let cool before removing from pan.

Just writing about the coffee hour makes me homesick for those old times in a peaceful world when the heart of the home beat in joyful rhythm to the music set by life itself, when every small happening was a note added to the great melody.

Yes, it was a different world, when countries knew very little about each other's patterns of life. Not so today.

In September, our garden plants that cannot stand the winter months have to be tended to. We must dig them up and replant them in pots to go into the house where they will bloom for us again during the dark months. Replacing them outdoors, tulip, hyacinth, and other bulbs will thrive through the winter and gladden our hearts in the spring. The only plants I take in are my geraniums, which have bloomed so faithfully all summer around the birdbath. They seem to be the first plants to fall victim to the frost. I can remember coming out into my garden many a late September morning to find the beautiful red blossoms turned to an ugly black.

Always, when I take in my geraniums, a strange story comes to my mind. It is in a way a sad story, but it has an amusing side, too. Perhaps it could not happen in these times, even in my homeland, but it is a true story and it did take place in the countryside in northern Sweden when I lived there as a little girl.

Sven and Anna were real people with many of the same emotions as people today. And pride and tactlessness still exist and separate lovers now as they did then. This particular story has become a legend as the old people like to tell it to the young ones who are a part of a new generation of a modern, progressive Sweden. It shows how little it really takes to destroy love. It is as easy to shatter as a flower pot if handled carelessly.

Sven and Anna are both gone now. They lived out their lives in lonely bitterness, each in his own small house on opposite sides of the village. In Anna's window the geraniums bloomed all winter long, but no one ever saw one of those plants in Sven's window. In fact, he never even planted them in his garden; this plant was a reminder of things he did not want to think about.

It had all started so properly. He was not young and neither was Anna. She was a seamstress who had faithfully served her community altering and repairing clothes, and sometimes even making new ones. The story began when Sven came to her house for the first time to have a pair of pants shortened. Anna was new in the neighborhood then, having recently bought the small cottage on the knoll, and no one knew much about her or where she came from. She fixed Sven's pants good and proper, and he came back with more things to be altered or shortened. After all, a bachelor needed help in such matters.

Anna liked Sven. He was a nice-looking man with strong, even, white teeth and a splendid crop of light brown hair. He was quite talkative, too, and with each visit he stayed a little longer. Anna invited him for afternoon coffee. Then it became suppers and gradually Sven's visit became a standard thing in the village. People said that he was courting Anna, the seamstress, and it looked as though it would not be long before she would move her geraniums across the village to Sven's white stucco house surrounded by farmland.

Then one moonlit night when they sat in the hammock on Anna's porch, Sven indirectly mentioned marriage.

"Anna," he said, "I've been thinking. It's a long way to walk across the village and I like being with you. Have you ever thought of selling your place and moving over to my house?"

Anna blushed like a schoolgirl. "Oh, I've been thinking about it," she confessed. "I like your company, Sven, and I could add my furniture to yours and place my flowers on your window sills, and we would have a real cozy home together."

"I would like that," said Sven.

Then they were silent for a while. Sven held Anna's hand and squeezed it now and then, but they did not talk any more that evening.

Sven never missed a night at Anna's house. He no longer

needed to bring mending an excuse to visit. He knew he was welcome anyway.

It was on a late September night that he first mentioned Bertha.

"I am surprised, Anna, that you never married," he said. "With your looks and ability it seems that you should have been snapped up a long time ago."

Anna looked dreamily out at the garden. "There might be a story behind it, Sven," she said simply. "Each heart has a story."

"Yes," said Sven, "it is so. There is always a story when people reach our age and have never married."

"And what is your story, Sven?" asked Anna, moving a little closer to him.

Sven stared at the floor. "Anna, there is a story," he admitted. "Someday I will tell you about it, but not tonight. I always feel so sad when I talk about Bertha."

But it was not until the night that Sven helped Anna take the geraniums into the kitchen that he told her. They had worked well together, taking up each plant and placing it in its individual pot. They stood now on the kitchen windowsill, four plants in a row. One big one, still covered with blossoms, had been left on the round table on the porch because they could enjoy it more there.

They had finished dinner. Anna had outdone herself in the art of cooking and Sven was content.

"I think before Christmas we will get married, Anna," he suggested, as they settled down in the hammock. "I have had a soft spot in my heart for you since the first time I saw you. You were the first person who had ever reminded me of Bertha."

Anna trembled a little. "Was Bertha beautiful?" she asked.

"Yes, the most beautiful thing I had ever seen until I met you."

"Did you know her a long time?"

"Ten years. For ten years we spent most of our time together."

Anna sighed deeply. "Ten years is a long, long time, Sven. Why isn't she with you now?"

Sven bowed his head. "Bertha died," he said.

"Oh, Sven, I'm so sorry. That was too bad."

Sven's arm was around her waist and he drew her close. "It is your eyes, Anna," he said, "and the way you look at me—even the way you hold your head and stretch your neck. Oh, it is as if I am seeing Bertha all over again."

Anna drew away from his embrace. "Perhaps the memory of her would always stand between us, Sven. Perhaps I could never fill her place in your life."

Sven began to laugh. He pulled Anna to him again and held her tight.

"No, Anna, that could never happen. How foolish I've been! I've never explained to you about Bertha, and I never realized until now that you didn't know who Bertha was when I talked about her. She could never have been what you are to me. Why, now I could even replace her. I never thought I'd be able to, but with you beside me, I could do it."

Anna stared at Sven and stammered, "I d-don't even k-know now wh-what you're talking about."

"But you will, Anna, my dearest. You see, Bertha was my horse, the finest animal that ever lived."

There was a heavy silence for a moment. Then Anna stood up, her eyes shooting flames. She glared at Sven, her face red and her voice filled with contempt.

"So that is what she was—this Bertha—a horse—a beautiful horse that looked just like me. And to think, Sven, that I was jealous of her, that I envied the love you felt for her! But now I understand clearly . . . I look like her . . . a perfect horseface . . . my eyes, my expression, my neck . . . I have all of it. But it's not for you, Sven. You go home with the memories of your precious Bertha and cherish them until the day you die. I'll never be a part of your life. Now get out of my house and never set foot in it again."

Sven stood up and moved toward Anna, intending perhaps to calm her, but too late. Already the big flower pot of blooming geraniums had been hurled at him and if he had not ducked, he might never have lived to tell the story, for the pot broke into a dozen pieces and so did its beautiful flowers.

No one ever saw Sven walk to Anna's home again. Their romance was over. In her house the sewing went on as before, and the geraniums bloomed in endless profusion. She never mentioned Sven to anyone. It was he who told the story. But no geraniums were ever seen on his property and all the village people knew why.

When I heard the story, I took Sven's side. I could understand how a lonely man could love his horse that much, but no one seems to share my logic. Love is a strange thing—whether it is of our time or way back in the yesteryears. And I am sad when a romance breaks up, for I like to believe that love is meant to last forever.

September is a good month for catching up on delayed invitations. It is a perfect time to entertain. It is neither too hot nor too cold, and we sort of get a second wind after the humid weather is gone. I also feel that in September I must start to get my house in order. Summer does a job on it and with a lot of helpful guests in the kitchen things sometimes become misplaced. So I begin with the kitchen closets and cupboards and drawers, taking a few a day, and when all those are done, I do the flat silver and put the pieces away all shiny again. This is a prelude to the heavier fall cleaning, and I enjoy getting back to indoor chores again, especially cooking and planning menus.

And so to a menu for this month of September.

ENTREE

Kåldormar

Baked potatoes   Mixed vegetables
Celery sticks   Dill pickles   Lingonberries
                Oatmeal bread

DESSERT

Banana cake

Coffee   Milk

KÅLDORMAR

1 large head of cabbage with loose leaves	1 slice stale bread
	½ cup bouillon
4 thick slices of Bermuda onion	1 pound hamburger
	1 teaspoon salt

½ teaspoon white pepper	1 stick of margarine
½ teaspoon sugar	2 tablespoons of butter
¼ teaspoon allspice	2 tablespoons of flour
1 egg	2 tablespoons of heavy
1 cup cooked rice	cream

Remove the large leaves whole from the cabbage and boil in water for five minutes. Set aside.

Chop the Bermuda onion and fry in butter.

Soak the bread in the bouillon.

Mix the hamburger with the bread and bouillon. Add onions, salt, pepper, sugar, allspice, egg, and rice. Work together until well mixed.

Put about two tablespoons of the mixture inside each cabbage leaf. Roll tightly and fasten with a toothpick.

Place one stick of margarine in a frying pan and fry the *kåldormar* until golden brown on each side. Place them side by side in a greased baking pan with 2 tablespoons of butter. Pour the fat from the frying pan over the *kåldormar.* Bake in a 300° oven for about 75 minutes.

Make a gravy by adding a little water to the drippings and thickening with 2 tablespoons of flour (mixed with a little water until smooth). Salt to taste. When thickened, add 2 tablespoons heavy cream.

Pour over *kåldormar* and serve.

MIXED VEGETABLES

Use frozen mixed vegetables. When cooked, add 2 tablespoons butter and a little Accent and salt. Mix lightly.

Select Idaho baking potatoes, wash well, and wrap in foil. Bake at 450° for 1 hour.

Wash and scrape celery. Keep cool and crisp until ready to serve.

OATMEAL BREAD

2 cups rolled oats
3 cups all-purpose flour
2 tablespoons butter
 (melted)
4 tablespoons sugar

2 teaspoons salt
2 cups milk (warmed)
2 packages of yeast dissolved
 in ¼ cup warm water

Mix rolled oats with flour. Add butter, sugar, and salt to warm milk. Add dissolved yeast. Stir in oats and flour and beat thoroughly. Cover and set in a warm place to rise until triple in bulk. Roll out on baking board dusted with flour into two large loaves (or if preferred three smaller ones). Use loaf pans for baking; time for large loaves 60 minutes in 350° oven, for smaller loaves about 50 minutes.

When bread is ready, it should be nicely browned and the loaf should be separated from the pan.

BANANA CAKE SUPREME

2 eggs (beaten)
2 cups sugar
6 mashed bananas (very
 ripe)
1 cup butter (melted)
2 teaspoons soda (dissolved
 in a little boiling water)

1 teaspoon cinnamon
1 teaspoon cloves
1 teaspoon nutmeg
3½ cups cake flour
1 large pinch salt
1 cup raisins
1 cup chopped nuts

Beat the eggs until light and fluffy. Add sugar and beat again. Add the melted butter and stir vigorously. Add the mashed bananas and soda. In a separate bowl, sift together the flour, salt, cinnamon, cloves, and nutmeg. Fold this mixture into the wet batter. Dust the raisins and chopped nuts with a little flour and add to the mixture.

Bake in a 350° oven about 55 minutes. Let cool. Spread hot vanilla glaze over the top of the cake, allowing it to drip down the sides.

VANILLA GLAZE

2 cups confectioner's sugar (sifted)
3 tablespoons milk
2 tablespoons butter
½ teaspoon vanilla

Measure the sifted confectioner's sugar into a pan. Heat with milk and butter over low heat, stirring constantly until smooth. Stir in vanilla.

September is now fading into eternity, taking the last of this year's summer with it. It has been a gentle month, preparing us for the cold weather and the bareness that will soon settle over the garden. I am grateful for its many golden days and even for its rain, and as it departs, I feel like reaching out my hand, as to an old friend who must leave just when we have begun to enjoy each other's company.

In my heart I bless September and, bidding it good-by, I brace myself for the future months. Just like life, I think. We don't like to let go of the autumn years of our lives. Rather than face old age, we cling to those good years and we forget that our wonderful Creator has promised us a beautiful sunset in the garden of life if we love and trust Him with all our hearts. We must follow the pattern of life, year by year, but to us is given the fortitude to meet each new day.

GOLD NUGGET:
In a small notebook write down the beautiful things that happen to you, and when you are low, take it out and read it. Your spirits will be lifted to heights unknown.

❧10

Dear God,

In this month of October the beauty of the earth must be a little bit like Heaven. With all my heart I thank Thee for the trees that flaunt their brilliance against the sky. There are times at twilight when I behold these magnificent colors that my soul grows homesick for eternity and the perfection that exists where Thou art. I pray for all the world—that it will stop its madness and proclaim that Thou art God and that, in spite of men, Thou art the ruler. Forgive us our erring ways and help us to repent. Give us goodness so that truth will fill our lives and we will reach out our hands to our fellow men in trust and love and understanding. Amen.

AMERICA has the most beautiful autumn of any country in the world. In most of Europe the fall is rainy and cold and gray, but in our great land the sun seems to love to shine and illuminate lavishly all the colors of nature. Its rays still warm the earth and the trees are so breathtakingly lovely in their multi-colors that it would be impossible to choose the most beautiful.

I love to travel in October, especially through the northern states of New Hampshire and Vermont. How well I remember a few years back when I had to drive from Plattsburg, New York, to Caribou, Maine. The road took me across Vermont and New Hampshire with the White Mountains in the distance. It was in the midst of the scarlet of fall, and it was so beautiful that at times it seemed my heart could not take in any more loveliness. And because I had to give voice to my feelings, I said to Jim Charles, "Have you ever seen anything so magnificent! I feel like running up mountains and jumping over stumps and streams. I wish I could sing so that I could burst my lungs. That is how happy I am!"

Of course, Jim Charles did not answer because he is just a one-eyed toy camel who sits on my dashboard. His full name is James Charles Brown and I picked him up in a little gift shop on a mountainside. Originally I bought him for my second grandson, Gary, who was a baby at the time. But as I was driving home, I placed Jim Charles in the front window and he fitted there so perfectly and he so endeared himself to me that I decided he would always accompany me as I traveled along unknown roads. Little Gary was given another toy and Jim Charles became my silent companion. I have changed automobiles many times since then, but the little toy camel always sits in the same spot. We have traveled thousands of miles together and when I need to open my heart and talk aloud, my little friend is a patient listener.

Perhaps my voice is heard most often when I behold something so beautiful that I cannot possibly contain myself. And viewing the splendor of fall is one of those times. October is a month when the woodland is enchanting with purplish-reds, golds, and crimsons, and the whole countryside looks like a fairyland. And when dusk descends on the forest, the sky becomes like velvet, soft and mellow, and the stars hang in a blue-gray mist. Later the night turns cold and the frost man comes around with his hatchet to see what he can destroy. But the trees in the forest keep their loveliness until the rain and strong winds tear at their leafy crowns. They show off their rainbow party dresses as if they are trying to capture all the beauty of the world in just one short month. They exhibit for us the autumn colors that we love and that many of us travel miles and miles to view.

Then suddenly, one morning, after the rain and wind have shaken them, the hillside trees appear in common brown. They have begun to undress and when October has passed, they stand there in their nakedness, partly concealed by the thick gray fog that proclaims the end of the season. Yet the trees will survive the long, cold winter, and I like to think that inside their bark there beats a heart which will welcome spring's return, although it now seems far away.

It is like life, I think, as I walk softly across the golden carpet where the aspen and birch have spilled their leaves. As we go, full of years, toward the autumn of our earth life, we, too, perhaps want to flaunt the last colors within our souls. We beg the fog and gray mist to hold off a little longer. The storms come, however, and we are shaken and cold, for, as old age approaches, we grow tired and frail. But time flows by and, satisfied with our years, we close our eyes and go to sleep. When we open them again, we behold the glory of eternity and unending spring.

The home holds many different moods within its heart, and sorrow and joy interchange. One day death will knock at the door and demand that loved one who has been an essential part of our lives. Then we must not fear or tremble, but reach up and find a hand reaching down to give us strength and comfort.

When our parents grow old and are ready to leave this earth, being ripe for eternity, we can visualize them slipping off an earthly garment and putting on a new celestial robe. The parting is not easy; tears will flow. But there must be no bitterness in our hearts because we sorrow not as those who have no hope. We shall meet again in a perfect world where we will never part.

But when the black angel takes our young and middle-aged at an untimely hour, how often we rebel and storm at God and demand "Why?" We forget that God's way is not our way and His thoughts are not our thoughts. And who are we to lift our voices toward the Almighty, demanding an explanation? How easily we forget that our minds are finite and that we can't understand fully the majesty and mystery of our Creator. We must learn to accept both life and death even as our hearts cry out in pain. In times of sorrow it is important not to let the home life sag, not to let ourselves take the attitude that we don't care or that things do not matter. This is not the right heartbeat for a home. No, let us force that smile and perform our household duties with poise and dignity in honor of those who trusted and loved us. Now more than ever the family needs nutritious meals and an attractively set table with delicious, appetizing foods.

I believe that the spirits of dear ones who have departed still linger among us and that the wall between life and death is very thin. To me there is no strangeness in this. I remember that after Mama left us and my heart ached with grief, I used to try to smile and call out into the unknown: "How am I doing? Are you pleased with me?"

In that way I could get hold of myself and keep up my daily routine.

In Sweden, food plays a big part at funerals. Invitations are sent out and a dinner is usually served at a hotel. After the graveside service, relatives and friends follow the sorrowing family home and coffee and elaborate refreshments are served. This fellowship helps to ease that first sting of loneliness. But eventually the people leave and the sorrow remains, for food and fellowship cannot erase the longing to hear those well-known footsteps or the sound of that sweet voice. And we have to learn that sorrow as well as joy is very much a part of the home.

Every home has memories tucked away in its shadows. Some are light; some are dark. Some are surrounded with laughter, others with tears. We can turn back time whenever we choose to live those memories over again. They can last a fleeting second or minutes or hours, but how very empty life would be without them. I would like to share one of my own memories, one that had almost been forgotten, it happened so long ago. It seemed strange that it should suddenly be brought back to life.

It happened on one of my speaking tours. It was October. I was in Muskegon, Michigan, and a guest in a lovely home. The hostess and I were having a cup of coffee in the living room when her youngest daughter came bouncing into the room. She was about ten years old—blonde, and with a twinkle in her blue eyes that made you feel that you had always known her. But my eyes did not stay on her face. It was her feet that I stared at and the shoes she was wearing. At first I could not believe my eyes, but it was true. She was wearing a pair of shoes that dated back to the late 1800's. I myself had once owned a pair like that. They were high black patent leather shoes with tiny black buttons halfway up the calf of her leg. They were very pointed and so narrow that one wondered that there was room for toes.

"I am wearing these shoes in your honor, Mrs. Bjorn," she said. "They come from Sweden and belonged to my great aunt. You see, we are Swedish on Mother's side. Her Aunt Selma willed these to me and I just adore them."

"How nice of you," I said. "They come from Sweden all right and I could not believe my eyes when you first came into the room."

The girl strutted around, anxious to show off her treasure. I smiled mechanically, but a lump began to fill my throat. I could have told a story about a pair of shoes like that, but I didn't, for even after all the years that memory brought me pain. I was to give a humorous talk in a couple of hours and I decided that I had better forget about the shoes and stay in a good mood.

But much later that evening, when the lecture was over and I had retired to a very comfortable and especially

130

lovely room where all was still and peaceful, I took the memory out.

I must have been about eleven years old, I reflected. It was October and darkness and cold had settled over the land. Eight children in one family could be quite a problem to feed and clothe and it was hard for Papa at times to make his money go around, especially when it was time to buy shoes for so many. In the summer we all ran barefoot, but as soon as fall arrived, out came the long black wool stockings and the heavy shoes. I hated the stockings. If you did not pull them up real tight, they made several rings around your leg. They were ugly, and the shoes were not exactly pretty either. But they were much better than the stockings.

Then one day a tragedy occurred. A sweet old lady, a member of Papa's church, came calling one afternoon at the parsonage with a large paper bag.

"I brought these shoes along," she said to Mama. "They are almost new, but they are too small for me, and I wonder if your oldest girl could wear them?"

They tried the shoes on me, and they were a perfect fit. Papa and Mama thanked her profusely and I had to say thank you too, but it was the blackest day in my young life. Papa told me I was to wear those shoes to school for the next season. I was a sensitive child, and the shoes were outmoded. No one ever wore shoes like those any more; pointed toes were completely out of style. I could not sleep a wink that night. My mind dwelt on just one thing. I could see myself walking into the schoolyard and all the children laughing at me and my silly shoes.

But Papa had spoken, and his orders were never disobeyed.

I prayed that night that I would die. I even told God that I wouldn't mind going to Hell; it would be a lot better than going to school in those shoes. But I did not die, and morning always follows even the darkest night. The tears ran down my cheeks, but neither Papa nor Mama seemed to notice them. There was no use begging; Papa would never change his mind.

I took the paper bag containing my lunch and started off toward school. My sisters and brothers ran ahead of me, fooling and laughing. They had no problems; their shoes were normal. They had nothing to be unhappy about. I rebelled and stormed in my heart. If God were so good, how I wished He had not picked me to shower this gift on. But I was the chosen one and I was about to face the worst day of my life. I looked down at my feet. The shoes looked horrible and reached almost to my knees. My toes seemed to be all cramped together and there was no room to wiggle them. I walked slowly. A light fog hung in the air. The spiders had spun their invisible ropes across the road and they caught on my face. I hated spiders. I hated the fog and school and the whole world. But I did not quite dare to hate Papa or Mama or God.

There was a brook gurgling along the roadside and it somehow seemed to call to me. The noise of the water blended with that storm within me, and before I knew it I was sitting at the edge of the road. In the distance I could hear the school bell ringing. I didn't care. I couldn't go to school that day; I just couldn't. It was too late to go then anyway. I would just sit there by the side of the brook. I would sit there all day until the children came home from school. I would do that every day until the teacher contacted my home to find out why I was missing. The thought of having postponed going to school for even a few days lightened my heart a little. I would not think of what would happen after that, but for a few days I was safe.

The morning was cold. I ate my lunch and threw the bag into the brook. I was lonely. It was as if no one in the whole world cared for me. Then an idea came to my mind. It was not the right thing to do, but I had done so much wrong already that one more sin could not matter too much. Papa always said that God did not count the sins; He weighed them. I hoped this last one would not weigh too much. It did not take long to carry out my plan and there I was—sitting in the brook. I was soaked—clothes, shoes, and all—and the water was ice cold. I stayed there only a moment and then I climbed out of the water, drenched. For the first time since I had received the gift of the shoes I laughed. I laughed because I realized how silly I must look. Of course, I could not possibly go to school under the circumstances. Already my brain was working overtime making up a perfect story of how I had gone too close to the brook, slipped, and fallen in; it was as simple as that.

Very likely I would be ill from dunking myself in that ice-cold water. Perhaps I would be sick in bed for a long time. Papa and Mama would feel sorry for me. Maybe I would be sick for a whole year. Then I would not need to go to school and I would outgrow the shoes. That thought made me happy and warm inside, although my body was shivering. I would make Papa believe that I was really sick; then at the opportune time I might even eat some pickled beets and spit them up, so he would think I had consumption or something; I had heard Mama say that to spit blood was very dangerous. Next summer Papa would have to pay someone to tutor me so I could go along with my class. I laughed out loud. Papa would have to pay for those shoes in the end.

I began my journey home, but my shoes were full of water. I thought I had better empty them first, so again I sat on the bank and took off my shoes and stockings. I had to wring out my stockings so I placed both my shoes beside me on the wilted grass. It was hard to wedge my wet feet into them again. Finally one shoe was on my foot, but as I reached out to pick up the other, I hit it with my hand and it tumbled down the bank right into the brook. To my horror, the stream took it and carried it away. I was stunned. Now how could I tell my story? Papa would never believe me. A buttoned shoe could not fall off even if I tumbled into the water. But I was shaking from the cold. Regardless of the consequences, I had to go home. I cried all the way until it seemed as if I had cried out all my tears. I didn't dare go inside, so I sat on the doorstep, where Mama found me.

She did not ask questions, but got me into bed, covered me with blankets, and poured hot milk and honey down my throat. I never had to explain. I was sick for weeks, so I never had to fool Papa. All they wanted was for me to get well. My parents must have pieced the story together and they must have understood, for I never saw that other shoe again. When I was well enough to go to school, a new pair of shoes was waiting for me. I knew they had forgiven me, and I asked God to forgive me, too. Somehow I had a feeling that God understood and had been on my side the whole time. I never held it against Papa; he never knew how hurt I had been inside. To him, a pair of shoes was a pair of shoes and if they fit you, you wore them. And Mama would never contradict Papa.

I went to sleep that night in Muskegon and dreamed that I was lecturing and when I looked down at my feet, I was wearing those high-buttoned patent leather shoes, which belonged to the little girl in whose house I was staying. But there was no pain connected with them . . . and no one laughed. This was a different era and a new generation and the shoes were a novelty. Still when I awoke the next morning, I was glad it was just a dream. There was no gloom in my heart even though I still think it strange that those shoes caught up with me after all those years.

October is such a busy month in the home. We have to pack away all our summer clothes, and bring out the fall outfits. Suddenly we think we have nothing to wear and start out on a shopping trip from store to store looking for a particular dress we have already seen in our mind. We try on felt hats, and after we have tried on a dozen different styles, we go back and buy the first one. But it is exciting to mill among the crowd, to window-shop, buy, and exchange, finally finding satisfaction in our purchases.

Then we must start our fall house cleaning. If we did a thorough job in the spring, we can cheat a little here and there, but work is still plentiful. Storm windows replace screens and awnings are pulled up to let the sunshine in. October seems to vanish before we know it.

We might even invite guests from out of town to come for a weekend. I just love weekend visitors. It is such a joy to plan and prepare things to wait for those welcome faces, to sit down and talk about the things that have happened since we were together last year. Perhaps they will arrive late on a Saturday night and we will drive to the airport to pick them up, so our meals do not begin until Sunday morning. We get up a little earlier to fix breakfast, having it ready about nine o'clock so we can all go to church together.

OUR BREAKFAST MENU:

Honeydew melon with frosted grapes
French toast with maple syrup
Crisp bacon
Coffee

Cut a melon in desired sizes and fill each with seedless grapes which have been dipped in beaten egg white, rolled in sugar, and laid on a paper towel to dry.

Before starting the French toast, fry or broil the bacon over medium heat, turning often. Drain on a paper towel and place in a baking pan in a 200° oven until the toast is ready. Then serve with the toast.

FRENCH TOAST

white bread	a dash of salt
3 eggs	¼ lb. butter
1 cup milk	

136

Trim the crusts from bread, allowing at least two slices per person.

Beat eggs; add milk and beat again. Add salt. Soak the bread thoroughly in this mixture. In a frying pan, melt ¼ pound of butter and brown lightly. Fry the bread in it, two or three slices at a time, until brown and crisp. Add more butter if needed.

DINNER

Orange juice with lemon sherbet
Party crackers
Roast leg of lamb
Roasted potatoes   French-cut wax beans   Harvard beets
Pear-and-cream-cheese salad
Mint jelly   Celery and Olives   Miniature gherkins
Vienna blue cheese bread
Butter balls

DESSERT

Pineapple cream pie
Mixed nuts   Mints
Coffee   Tea

For your appetizer, use one pint of orange juice and ½ pint lemon sherbet. Mix it in a blender on high speed for three minutes and serve.

ROAST LEG OF LAMB

1 leg of lamb	1 teaspoon paprika
1 tablespoon baking soda	1 cup black coffee
5 tablespoons flour	1 cup beef bouillon
1 teaspoon salt	3 small onions (sliced)

Rub baking soda on the lamb and let stand for 10 minutes. Wash thoroughly. Sprinkle 3 tablespoons flour in the bottom of a roasting pan and place the lamb in the pan. Sprinkle salt and paprika over the lamb and dust with the remaining 2 tablespoons flour.

Preheat the oven to 450°. Roast meat for 30 minutes. Remove from oven and pour the coffee over the lamb. Roast for 10 more minutes. Remove and pour bouillon over lamb. Place sliced onions around it in the pan. Turn the oven down to 300° and roast, allowing 20 minutes per pound. Baste the lamb occasionally. If it becomes too dry, add water. When fully cooked, remove potatoes and lamb from the roasting pan and make a gravy from the drippings.

GRAVY

drippings	1 cup water
1 teaspoon Gravy Master	½ teaspoon sugar
3 tablespoons flour	salt to taste

To the drippings add Gravy Master. Dissolve the flour in the water; stir until smooth. Let the drippings come to a boil and add flour mixture. Boil until thick. If there is not enough of the drippings, add bouillon. Strain the gravy and add sugar and salt. Put gravy in a double boiler and whip until shiny. Keep the water in the bottom of the double boiler at a slow boil to keep the gravy piping hot.

ROASTED POTATOES

Select as many small round potatoes as needed. Wash and peel. Three quarters of an hour before the meat is ready, place the potatoes in the roasting pan. Salt lightly. Turn the potatoes every 10 minutes to brown them evenly.

WAX BEANS FRENCH STYLE

Wash beans and snip off ends. Cut lengthwise with a sharp knife (each bean in about three slices.) Place in boiling water and salt lightly. Boil slowly for 15 minutes or until tender. Drain and add 2 tablespoons butter, a dash of salt, and Accent.

HARVARD BEETS

¼ cup vinegar
3 cups cubed cooked beets
2 tablespoons butter
2 tablespoons flour

1¼ cups hot water
1 teaspoon salt
⅛ teaspoon pepper

Heat vinegar and pour over beets in a bowl. Let stand for 10 minutes. Melt butter and add flour, mixing to a smooth paste. Add hot water to the paste and cook until thick, stirring constantly. Remove the beets and add the vinegar to the sauce. Add salt and pepper. Pour sauce over the beets and serve.

PEAR-AND-CREAM-CHEESE SALAD

Select large canned pears and drain off the syrup. Form the cream cheese into balls and roll each one in chopped pecans. Put a cream cheese ball in the hollow of each pear. Place on a lettuce leaf.

Mix 1 tablespoon pear juice with 3 tablespoons mayonnaise. Add a drop of green vegetable coloring and stir. Spoon over salad before serving.

VIENNA BLUE CHEESE BREAD

1 long loaf Vienna bread
1 package blue cheese butter

Cut the bread (entire loaf) lengthwise. Butter each half generously and spread on the blue cheese thickly. Wrap in foil and warm in a 200° oven about 20 minutes. Slice in thick pieces and serve.

BUTTER BALLS

Roll small pieces of butter between two flat wooden paddles until they form perfect balls. Heap in a butter dish and garnish with parsley.

PINEAPPLE CREAM PIE

1 cup water	¾ cup sugar
2 tablespoons butter	1 cup crushed pineapple
2 tablespoons cornstarch	2 egg yolks (beaten)

Bring the water and butter to a boil, and pour over the cornstarch and sugar which have been stirred together. Cook for 15 minutes, stirring constantly. Cool the mixture, stirring while cooling. Add pineapple and reheat. Remove from the heat. Add a tablespoon of the mixture to the beaten egg yolks and stir (to warm the egg yolks). Then stir the egg yolks slowly into the mixture and beat until cool. Chill.

Pour into a baked pie shell (page 93) and cover with topping. Do not bake after filling.

TOPPING

1 cup whipping cream   3 tablespoons confectioner's sugar
½ teaspoon vanilla

Whip cream. Add sugar and vanilla and spread over pie.

Our company might stay until late Sunday evening, so we will have to plan a light supper.

Broiled open-faced cheese, bacon, and tomato sandwiches
Half a peach fill with cottage cheese
Potato chips
Chocolate cake
Coffee   Milk   Cocoa

SANDWICHES

Butter as many slices of white bread as needed. Spread each generously with a cheddar cheese spread; top with two thin slices of tomato and two half slices of bacon. Broil under a low flame until the bacon is cooked and the sandwich nicely browned. Serve at once.

SALAD

Fill a peach half with cottage cheese and place beside the sandwich along with potato chips. Garnish with parsley.

CHOCOLATE CAKE

½ cup butter	1¾ cups cake flour
1½ cups sugar	1 teaspoon soda
2 eggs	½ teaspoon salt
2 squares unsweetened baking chocolate (melted)	1 cup milk
	1 teaspoon vanilla

Cream the butter. Add sugar and beat. Beat eggs and add to the mix. Beat until light and fluffy. Add chocolate and put aside. In a separate bowl sift the flour, soda, and salt. Fold into the mixture alternating with milk. Add vanilla. Pour into a greased square baking pan. Bake at 350° 40–50 minutes.

Cool cake completely before frosting.

FROSTING

2 tablespoons melted butter	2 tablespoons heavy cream
2 squares baking chocolate (unsweetened) melted confectioner's sugar	1 teaspoon vanilla

Combine the butter and chocolate; add cream and mix vigorously. Add enough confectioner's sugar to make the frosting the right consistency for spreading. Add the vanilla last.

Entertaining is such a gracious part of life, and it lends so much warmth, dignity, and fun to the home. It is also exciting to be a guest and to spend a weekend with friends. Then it is your turn to be waited on. If you want to have friends, you must be one. If you want to be invited, you must invite; that is the law of the home.

Soon this lovely month of October will be over, a month filled with beauty, life, and activity. God has created the months with such variety. How different they are, each one giving to us something that only it can give. And our hearts should be grateful.

GOLD NUGGET:

When the house is to be left empty for a couple of weeks, house plants can be kept from drying up by giving them a good watering before you go away. Then place a large basin of water in the room where all the plants are to be left. Shut the door to the room. The water will evaporate and the plants will draw moisture from the air.

◦11

Dear Heavenly Father,

We thank Thee for blessings which we have taken for granted, for love and happiness and for dear ones. We thank Thee for food that comes in such abundance from fields heavy with golden grain. We thank Thee for America, our land, where the Pilgrims came to find the freedom to worship, to serve, and to love Thee and all mankind with their innermost hearts.

We thank Thee for a faith with wings to lift us above evil and wrong to seek the truth. We thank Thee for prayer that builds bridges over the impossible and gives us visions that all things work together for good for those who love Thy name.

At this Thanksgiving season we stand in awe of Thy majesty and whisper, "How great Thou art!" Amen.

SWEDEN does not have a national Thanksgiving Day. America is the only country in the world that has such a day. There could not be a more beautiful beginning for a great nation than the Pilgrims' arrival, having dared the wind and cold of a stormy ocean to reach a shore where they could pray and worship the Lord God as their hearts directed. That privilege was so very, very precious, and God blessed their land. America has become a rich nation filled with people who immigrated here from the Old World because this was such a good land. It is still a good land, but not as it was. So often our people forget its beginning. That is why Thanksgiving Day, according to Presidential proclamation, is so important; actually every citizen should dedicate this whole month to counting his blessings.

November is a gray month; the brilliant autumn is over. But Thanksgiving Day gives it color and meaning. It is a day of memories of dear ones who used to sit with us around the dinner table. Each person has his own special memories. I can see Papa there at the head of our family's table, the big turkey in front of him, and Mama at the other end with all the other dishes, piping hot and ready to fill the children's plates. How much we as a family loved this day. Like a huge magnet it drew us all closer together. When we were of school age, it was the turkey and all the good food that we longed for. Later on, when one after another left for college, it was the anticipation of seeing everyone again that made the day so joyful. And they came hundreds of miles, driving their dilapidated old cars that kept going more on prayer than on gasoline; but home they came, because no matter where they were in this big land, no place was dearer than home. As the years went by and we grown children had our own young

144

families, we saw the table get longer and longer and the turkey get larger and larger. Eventually some could no longer make it home for that holiday; the distance was too great. But we were thankful for those years that we had had as a family, for that is what Thanksgiving Day represents—home and loved ones, thanksgiving and togetherness. I pray that America will always have a Thanksgiving Day.

It is a worthwhile objective, to focus our thoughts from the very beginning of this month on all the things we have to be grateful for and to give our thanks to God with a joyful heart, especially for our country and all its bounty. I have two grandsons to be thankful for in this month. Gary, my second grandson, always carries goodness and sunshine with him. He is growing up now, already in his early teens, and I am very proud of him—a pride mingled with humility. How can a grandmother express her heart's feelings about such precious gifts as grandchildren? Last Thanksgiving little Christopher had not yet arrived. How we waited; we thought he would never come. But he did come two days after Thanksgiving, looking just like a little Beatle with many inches of soft black hair. "He's just keeping up with the styles," we said as we welcomed him into our family. When there has not been a tiny baby in a family for nine years, a new one is extra special. Christopher is our pride and joy; it is fun watching him grow into his own little person. And anything we do for him is rewarded with smiles, coos, and chubby little arms reaching out to hug. How grateful we are for babies; what a big place they fill in the heart of the home.

This is the wonder of growing old, seeing a new generation being born, growing up, and coming to power. How we pray that they will be strong and courageous and be great leaders for our land. That is why it is so important for homes to turn out good citizens, starting early to teach the little ones the difference between right and wrong and to practice honesty and integrity. And as we take inventory of our own lives, we must dedicate ourselves anew to truth and justice and brotherhood, so that the Lord will bless our nation and all the families within its boundaries.

Although we did not have a special Thanksgiving Day in Sweden when I was growing up, Mama invented days like that now and then. As I look back, I know that she connected much of the happiness of earth life with gratefulness. To be grateful for large and small things alike and to praise God for everything was really the secret of happiness. Mama told us many stories to anchor this thought in our minds. And I find myself, now that I am getting older, taking out one of Mama's stories to evaluate it anew so that I will never forget the precious secret of a happy life. One story which I have never forgotten is particularly appropriate in this Thanksgiving season. I shared it once in a little booklet on prayer, but it is well worth repeating.

Even though Mama taught us daily to be thankful, her stories seemed to make a greater impact on our minds. My grandmother had told Mama this story when she was a little girl. Since there was neither radio nor television in those days, parents told stories for enjoyment and to teach a lesson. To deal with the present and the future, I feel we need to swing back to some of those values of home life that, in the rush and bother of today, we have left behind.

In my mind's eye, I can still see Mama sitting back in the sofa, her blue eyes looking dreamily into the fire, while we children were gathered around her, our eyes wide with anticipation, our hearts ready to receive, keep, and ponder. Mama's voice always became mellow and tender as she began to tell a story:

This all took place over one hundred and fifty years ago when Sweden was at war and awful things were happening across the land. People were disheartened and fearful, and doors were bolted day and night against enemy soldiers who roamed about the countryside. No one was safe from harm.

Far from the village, in the hilly part of the country, an old woman lived in a small red cabin. Her home was very dear to her because it had belonged to her parents and their parents before them. It was an old, old house, but it had a bit of land, and the woman had a cow and a pig and some chickens. In the summertime she raised potatoes, carrots, and turnips. She even had a cabbage patch. All those vegetables she could store for the winter, and her cow gave her milk and the chickens laid eggs. When she slaughtered the pig in the fall, she always replaced it with a baby piglet so that she could salt down pork each fall. Although she had very little money, she felt she was well provided for and as she grew old and tired, she enjoyed the stillness and restfulness that surrounded her life. Every day she offered up her thanksgiving to the Lord God for His goodness to her.

One day in November as she was finishing her chores in the barn, a soldier came galloping up the road on a black horse. He rode right into her back yard, and the news he carried was not good.

"A whole battalion of enemy soldiers is marching up the road," he shouted. "They've plundered and murdered wherever they've found a dwelling. If they march all night, they should reach your home in the early morning hours, and I've come to warn you."

"But what am I to do?" asked the woman. "I'm old and frail and here alone. All I have is my cow and pig and chickens. If the soldiers took those away from me, I would have nothing."

"They certainly will take them," said the soldier, "and your own life is in danger. I advise you to take some heavy blankets and walk deep into the woods and remain there until the danger is over."

And after asking for water for his horse, the soldier galloped away to warn other farmers up the road. The woman stood there looking after him, her heart heavy with fear.

But a little while after the soldier had gone, she got hold of herself. As she looked up into the blue November sky, her faith in God welled up within her and suddenly the fear disappeared. She went into her cabin and took out her big worn old Bible and sat down to read it. For a long, long time she sat there reading and she found in the book promise after promise that the Lord God had made to mankind who put their trust in Him.

As dusk began to fall over the countryside, she went out to the barn again and milked her cow. She patted its soft, brown nose and gave it an extra tap of hay and plenty of water. She went to the pig sty and gave a double amount of mush to the pig; she fed the chickens plenty of grain. Then she gathered up the eggs, took her pail of milk, went into her house, and bolted the door. After she had eaten her supper, she knelt by her bed and poured out a prayer of thanksgiving, not asking, just thanking God that she had His promise to protect her from the wicked soldiers. She prayed for her animals, too, and then she went to bed.

The old woman fell into a sound sleep, and she had a strange dream, in which she saw a band of angels holding hands, forming a large ring around her house. It was a happy dream and she slept until daylight. But when she sat up in her bed and looked out the window she could see nothing. She tried to open the door, but found that a heavy snowfall had blocked it. So she said her morning prayers, put more wood in the stove, and got the house nice and warm. The coffee was brewing and as she was having her breakfast, it seemed to her that the band of angels was still there, surrounding her little cabin.

It was late afternoon before the sun finally began to melt the snow enough so that she could push the door open and get out to the barn. How glad she was that her pets had been given that extra food the night before. Of course, it had been hard for the cow to store all that milk, but now the old lady had so much milk that she could splurge a little to celebrate the protection given her by her wonderful Heavenly Father.

Later she learned that it had begun to snow right after dark the day before. Snow was not unusual in November in this part of Sweden, but people said they had never seen such big snowflakes. They seemed to come down in sheets and they covered everything in sight. By midnight the wind had begun to blow and the snow had drifted into a high wall between the old lady's house and the road. The soldiers had marched up the road in the early morning; some houses had been looted and the people had had to run out and hide wherever they could find shelter, but the soldiers had not seen her cabin and the little barn behind it. They had been shielded by the high wall God had built in front of the little red cabin. Never had a soul been more grateful to God who looks after his own.

Here Mama would stop and look at us, the love in her eyes making us aware that we were more precious to her than anything else.

"Children," she said, "don't ever forget this story. Carry it with you through life and remember that no danger is too great for your Lord God's protection if you pray in faith with thanksgiving."

This story often comes back to me at Thanksgiving time, as I remember the many occasions during my lifetime when the road has been rough and I have had to lean on those promises. I pray that, as my children look back into their childhood, they too will remember how I always tried to instill in them a faith in God that holds even in a time of atomic bombs and of evil. God's arm is never too short to reach down and help, to give us perfect security. He can even build walls of safety, and we can sleep without fear or worry when we trust and obey Him.

The other day when my younger daughter was home with me, we were talking about this November chapter.

"Please, Mother, when you write your recipes for this month, tell how to roast a turkey," she said.

I had to think for a moment.

"I did not plan to write about the Thanksgiving dinner at all," I told her. "For this month I wanted to suggest a light meal—an omelet and a spinach salad that I just love."

"You can talk about those, too, but so many of us young housewives get confused when it comes to roasting a turkey. We need to know, step by step, a sure way, and your turkeys are so good."

Well, finally I gave in, telling her I would have my omelet and spinach salad, too. So we have these extra items this month.

I'll never forget how I got the recipe for this spinach salad. I was on a speaking tour in Indiana, and there I had the privilege of staying with the son of a dear friend of mine. This friend and I used to wheel our babies together when we were neighbors in Springfield, Massachusetts. Her Donald and my Shirley were about the same age, and whenever the sun shone even in the cold of winter, we took long walks with our infants. They were our first and this tied us together in a strong friendship that has lasted through the years. Now Donald was a professor and had an adorable wife and the cutest children. And here I was enjoying myself in their lovely home. There was to be an addition to their family momentarily and Nancy was just waiting to dash off to the hospital.

"I do hope that the baby waits until after your speech," she confided. "Just tonight and tomorrow so we can have this visit."

As I retired, I worried a little. Nancy should not have stayed up so late. Sure enough, in the early morning hours, Donald knocked at my door.

"Will you keep an ear open for the kids?" he asked. "I have to take Nancy to the hospital."

So I was shifted out for lunch that day. I went to a nice farm in the country and it was there I got this recipe:

SPINACH SALAD

Toss together:

6 cups spinach (uncooked)
½ Bermuda onion (sliced)
1 cup chopped celery
4 hard-boiled eggs (sliced)
½ teaspoon salt

Dressing

Blend together:

1 package garlic-cheese salad dressing
3 teaspoons lemon juice
1 cup sour cream

An omelet goes perfectly with this salad, and they make a very welcome light luncheon when the guests are dieting ladies.

FLUFFY OMELET

1 whole egg
5 eggs separated
½ teaspoon salt
1 small glass of currant jelly

½ teaspoon pepper
3 tablespoons water
¼ pound butter

Add the whole egg to the five egg yolks and beat until light and fluffy. Add salt and pepper and beat again. Put aside. Beat the egg whites until stiff, so they stand up in peaks. Set aside. Add water to the egg-yolk mixture and beat again until light. Melt the butter in a skillet. Tip the pan many times until the sides are thoroughly buttered. Keep on medium heat to keep the butter hot, but don't brown. Fold egg whites into the other mixture, slowly and lightly until it is all well blended. Pour into skillet and cook for 10 minutes. With a spatula loosen the sides of the omelet, and lift slightly from the bottom. Let cook another 10 minutes.

Place in the oven which has been heated to 300°. Let omelet bake for 6 minutes, then test with a toothpick. If it comes out dry, the omelet is ready.

Fold in half and fill with currant jelly. Serve immediately on a heated plate.

Serve with tiny broiled sandwiches.

TINY BIT BROILS

Remove the crusts from slices of white bread and cut each slice into triangular pieces. Butter and spread with a cheddar cheese spread topped with chopped bacon. Broil until the bacon is cooked. Serve hot.

Thanksgiving Day comes at the end of the month of November, and the weather is usually chilly. It is wise to prepare early for this festive day, and much of the work should be done beforehand so the hostess is not all tired out when relatives or other guests arrive. The house can easily be cleaned on Tuesday. Wednesday should be completely reserved for doing odds and ends. The table can be set, the place cards can be written, and the center-piece created and put in place. Chrysanthemums are beautiful at this time of the year, and they add a lovely touch to a room, but I like to use fresh fruit for a centerpiece. There is something about the aroma of bright red apples in a room that adds to the feeling of Thanksgiving. The apples should, of course, be polished to a lovely glow, and should be accompanied by bright yellow oranges and orange tangerines. The many different kinds and colors of grapes play a part in my art work, as do bananas and nuts. It is an easy centerpiece to make, and sets off the snowy white damask cloth and the neatly folded matching napkins. The silver has been newly polished and everything is perfect, with tall orange candles on either side of the fruit bowl. The last minute shopping has been done and the menu for the big day has been written down and placed on the kitchen counter to be checked off so nothing will be forgotten.

THANKSGIVING DAY FEAST

Fresh fruit cup
Roast turkey with gravy
Mashed potatoes Turnip Squash Onion casserole
Sweet gems   Green beans
Wedges of lettuce with Russian dressing
Cranberry sauce   Spiced crabapples
Watermelon pickles   Tiny dill pickles
Butterscotch rolls with butter balls

DESSERT

Favorite pies   Special ice-cream roll
Nuts   Fruit   Mints
Cider   Coffee

FRESH FRUIT CUP

3 oranges	1 package frozen melon balls
2 grapefruits	1 package frozen raspberries
20 grapes (seeded)	2 apples
2 bananas	6 maraschino cherries
1 fresh pineapple	6 mint leaves

Peel and cut oranges in small chunks. Do the same with the grapefruits. Place in bowl. Add the seeded grapes and sliced bananas. Peel and cut up pineapple and add to the other fruit. Thaw the melon balls and raspberries and add to the previous mixture. Last add the apples (peeled and chunked). Serve in sherbet cups and decorate with cherries and mint leaves.

It is best to make the turkey stuffing first and set it aside until the turkey is ready to be stuffed.

TURKEY STUFFING

gizzard mixture	1 teaspoon sage
1 pound margarine	1 tablespoon poultry dressing
2 loaves of stale white bread	1 large onion, finely chopped
(more or less, according to	2 stalks celery, finely chopped
size of turkey)	

Cook gizzard, heart, and liver in 2 cups water until tender. Chop and set aside.

Pour melted margarine over the bread and work by hand until well mixed. Add spices, onion, celery, and gizzard mixture and work until smooth. Do not salt.

Set aside.

ROAST TURKEY

Pick all the pinfeathers from the turkey and rub with baking soda. Let stand 10 minutes. Wash turkey well both inside and out and dry with a Turkish towel. Lightly salt the inside and let stand 5 minutes.

Stuff the bird. Tie in wings and legs with white string. Pin the back end and neck with stainless steel nails. Melt a chunk of butter and dip a clean cloth in it and go over the whole turkey with the butter. Salt lightly and sprinkle with a little paprika. Flour the turkey lightly and sprinkle 3 tablespoons flour in a roasting pan.

Heat the oven to 450°. Place turkey in oven and watch it closely. When it is well browned, turn heat down to 300°, cover top with foil, and roast, allowing at least 20 minutes per pound. When flour is brown in the bottom of the pan, add water and a couple of chicken bouillon cubes. Baste turkey every 10 minutes.

Plan to have it ready at least 30 minutes before dinner. Remove it to a platter and garnish with parsley.

GRAVY

Add to the hot turkey drippings, 3 tablespoons flour dissolved in a cup of water and stirred smooth. Boil until thickened. If there are not enough drippings, add water and a chicken bouillon cube (1 cube to 1 cup water). Salt to taste and add ½ teaspoon sugar. Strain the gravy into a double boiler (to keep it piping hot), add ¼ cup heavy cream and whip until shiny.

MASHED POTATOES

Select as many potatoes as needed and boil in salted water until done. Pour off water, cover, and let stand 3 minutes to dry. Add milk and butter according to need (¼ pound butter to 8 potatoes). Mash. Salt to taste. Keep hot by putting pan in another pan of boiling water.

TURNIPS

Cook turnips until tender. Drain. Add salt, butter, and Accent.

156

SQUASH

Prepare frozen squash as directed. Add butter, salt, pepper, and Accent.

GREEN BEANS

Use fresh green beans and cut into small pieces. Cook until tender, about 10 minutes, flavor with butter, salt, pepper, and Accent.

ONION CASSEROLE

Select small white onions, peel, and let come to a boil. Pour off the first water and cover onions again with salted water. Boil for 10 minutes. Drain. Place in a casserole dish and cover with cream sauce.

CREAM SAUCE

2 cups milk	a dash of sugar
2 tablespoons flour	diced cheese
¼ pound butter	breadcrumbs
salt to taste	additional butter
a dash of pepper	

Melt the butter over a low heat. Stir in flour to make a smooth paste. Add milk and stir. Add seasonings. Let it come to a boil.

Remove from the heat and pour over onions. Top with diced cheese, breadcrumbs, and dots of butter. Bake for 30 minutes in a 350° oven.

SWEET GEMS

Use canned yams and warm with 2 tablespoons butter. Place in a baking dish. Top with slices of apple and marshmallows. Bake in a 300° oven for 35 minutes.

SALAD

Cut iceberg lettuce into wedges and top with Russian dressing.

DRESSING

To 3 tablespoons mayonnaise, add 1 tablespoon chili sauce. Mix well.

BUTTERSCOTCH ROLLS

2 packages of yeast	1 cup warm milk
¼ cup sugar	3¼ cups flour
1 teaspoon salt	2 tablespoons melted
1 egg	butter
extra butter, chopped pecans, brown sugar	

Beat together the yeast, sugar, salt, egg, and milk. Add flour and butter. Let rise to double bulk (about 1 hour).

Into each muffin cup (2 dozen) put a small piece butter, 1 teaspoon brown sugar, 1 teaspoon chopped pecans.

Roll the dough into a rectangular shape ¼ inch thick. Spread with butter and sprinkle with sugar. Roll up lengthwise and cut into 24 pieces. Place one piece in each tin. Let rise until double size. Bake in a 400–415° oven for 15 to 20 minutes. When ready, tip onto a rack upside down.

These should be baked early on Thanksgiving morning.

For dessert you may use your favorite pie. Our family prefers ice cream after that big dinner, so I buy a fancy ice-cream roll.

No matter how festive the occasion and how well cooked the dinner, the most important part of Thanksgiving Day is the atmosphere. Every person should feel at home and more than welcome; everyone should be greeted with a hug and a warm handshake. If the household can radiate warmth and good fellowship as well as serve a perfect dinner, the day will glow in memory down the years.

So we close the chapter of the month of November with its memorial Thanksgiving Day, not in honor of men but in honor of God, not as gain for our own egos, but as an opportunity to share and to give and to be at peace with all mankind.

Most communities have a church service on that day so that families can attend to give thanks. It is lovely if the whole family can sit together in the pew, even on this busy day for the housewife. Sometimes it can be arranged if the dinner is served late in the afternoon. I love to have it at dusk, just when the day is beginning to end. The house smells of wonderful food; the candles on the table give off their warm glow; voices are happy and gay. Old and young, big and small, gather around the table as evening grace is said, and a touch of eternity lingers over a home. These are moments that millions of dollars could never buy.

There is very little need for another meal even if the guests stay late. Nothing fills a person quite as full as a Thanksgiving dinner. But we usually have a cold-turkey-sandwich snack before the guests leave, served, perhaps, with a cup of coffee and apricot bars, something sweet to top off the day.

APRICOT BARS

½ cup butter
¼ cup sugar
1 cup all-purpose flour (sifted)

Mix the above ingredients together and pack into the bottom of an 8x8 pan (greased). Bake 25 minutes in a 350° oven. (If you use a pyrex dish, bake at 325°.)

FILLING

⅔ cup dried apricots	¼ teaspoon salt
2 eggs	½ teaspoon vanilla
1 cup brown sugar	½ cup chopped nuts
⅓ cup sifted flour	confectioner's sugar
½ teaspoon baking powder	

Boil the apricots in as little water as possible until soft. Set aside.

Beat eggs well. Add brown sugar, flour sifted together with baking powder and salt. Add vanilla and fold in the apricots.

Spread on top of the baked mixture and sprinkle with nuts. Bake another 25 minutes until golden brown.

Cut in squares and roll in confectioner's sugar.

So the day is over and the guests have left. The house is still once more, but in a strange way the spirit of love and friendship lingers and even the happy voices seem to be very near. Husband and wife depart to the kitchen to survey the mess, for a mess it is. But it was worth it and now, together, they take hold and soon all is shipshape and they can sit down and relax. Of course they are tired, but it is a good tiredness because one's strength has been lovingly shared with others. Another Thanksgiving Day will come and a little prayer goes up to God that every chair will be filled and not one of the loved ones will be missing.

GOLD NUGGET:

By inviting a lonely stranger to the family feast, one sometimes entertains an angel as a guest.

❦12

Lord of Lords and King of Kings,

Our hearts sing because this month has within it Christmastime when love was born and when man saw, for the first time, the fullness of Thy Father love to Thine earth children. We saw the star! We journeyed to the stable and there we took the Christ child into our hearts, and as He grew to maturity we began to understand the miracle of it all. Our words are too small to praise Thee as we should; our voices too weak to shout our joy; our hearts too narrow to take in all that love. But, Lord, come again into our midst and set us free. Come among men with peace, among nations with good will. Come to our war-torn world with tolerance and mercy.

Forgive us if we have taken the wrong roads, if we have been blinded with hate against any of Thy creations. Let Thy light shine into our hearts and make us new beings that we may reap Thy peace. Amen.

WHEN the sheet of the calendar that was November thirtieth is torn off and December first comes into view, it creates an exhilarating feeling in my heart. It is going to happen again, I think. The miracle will take place—the world will give itself to the Christmas season. This is the most exciting time of the year and we need the whole month to attune our homes to it. To me, Christmas is not a day or a season, nor is it just buying gifts and wrapping presents, running from store to store at a mad pace, and getting all those Christmas cards out on time. No, it is the joy and gladness and blessing that come with understanding the real meaning of Christmas. It is love and charity and giving. It is thoughtfulness of others. It is that sparkle in children's eyes and the little sacrifices made to give a certain gift to a dear one. What can be compared to it? I thank God for Christmas as every year it becomes dearer and dearer to my soul. I pray that hatred and darkness will never put out the light of that star that glowed so many hundreds of years ago over the little town of Bethlehem.

Perhaps we underestimate the pleasure we derive from starting so many projects. To prepare for Christmas is a great privilege which takes precedence over all other tasks in December.

December mornings are crisp and cold, and our gardens are white with heavy frost. At dusk, the trees stand like silhouettes against the dark blue sky, and the stars are lit one by one in the firmament. This is the darkest time of the year, but the glow within us makes us forget the darkness, because we look forward to the many brilliant lights that will soon brighten our community and our home, and especially to the glowing star on each Christmas tree. No darkness can discourage us at this time of year.

The first days of the month must be spent in planning. It is helpful to put down on paper a list of things to be accomplished.

Let us start by carefully checking over the Christmas-card list. How sadly we discover that some names must be crossed off because of dear friends who have passed away. As one grows older, that particular list grows longer each year. But it is wonderful to know that these friends have no need of cards this year, for where they are, the lights shine forever. That is the first item on the agenda. Then it is wise to write the addresses on all the envelopes but save the greetings to do later. On some envelopes I put a star in the right-hand corner to indicate that I must write a note on the card before I seal it. Almost all of those that go to foreign lands and especially my own Sweden have stars in the corner right where the stamp will be placed. If I do all this early enough, I have time to read each verse, making sure it is appropriate for the family to which it is sent. It is good to do this before the big rush begins.

At times we complain that the card list gets longer and longer each year. But if I think of the people the cards go to, I stop sputtering. What a small price, I think, to pay for friendship. After all, isn't friendship one of the rarest things in the world? To spend a little time and money to send a greeting once a year to so many is but a small token for so much.

I used to get befuddled trying to find so many addresses

and trying to remember if I had sent a card the year before or if an address had changed. So one year I revolutionized my whole system. In an empty stationery box I placed plain recipe cards, as many as the names on my list. And I filled them in as follows:

	Sent	Year	Received
Mr. and Mrs. So and So	x	67	x
Number and Street	x	68	no
City, State, and Zip Code		69	
		70	
		71	
		72	
		73	
		74	
		75	
		76	

If there is a change of address, there is plenty of room to change it on the card, and I can keep track of a family for ten years with hardly any work at all.

Of course, I file the cards alphabetically, and this method surely saves time.

After the envelopes have been addressed, I begin to set my Christmas-gift list straight in my own mind. I make up one list for the family, allowing for the fact that I may change my mind many times before this is absolute. The second list is for friends. The third list is for acquaintances I feel I should remember, such as the mailman, the news boy, the milkman, our pastor's family, etc. And the fourth list is for charities I must not forget. Checks must be made out to the Salvation Army, the Bowery Mission, the Toy-for-Joy Fund, and so many others. Having organized this is a load off my mind, and now I can turn my thoughts to strictly household duties.

I still have until December 14 before I must begin baking my Christmas cookies. I never start baking until after Lucia Day. But I do make a list of the kinds of cookies I plan to bake so I won't forget any.

This year I shall bake:

Drömmar	*Strutar*
Finska Bröd (Yule Logs)	Fruit Goodies
Formar	Cornflake Macaroons
Kisses	Pecan Balls
Uppåkrakakor	*Peppar-kakor* (page 37)
Smörstjörnor	*Spritz* (page 37)
Jul-kakor	Chocolate Wafers (page 47)
Christmas *Kringlor*	

DRÖMMAR

2 cups butter	3 cups flour
2 cups sugar	
½ teaspoon ammoniated powder	

Cream the butter and add sugar and ammoniated powder. Work in the flour until you have a smooth dough. Grease a baking sheet and drop the dough onto it by the teaspoonful, about an inch apart. Bake in a slow oven, 300°, about 15 to 20 minutes until light brown. The cookies should be high and puffy. Don't remove them too soon or they may fall.

FINSKA BRÖD (YULE LOGS)

1 cup butter	1 tablespoon almond extract
1¾ cups flour	4 tablespoons sugar

Topping

1 beaten egg white   1 teaspoon green coloring
mixture containing equal amounts sugar and chopped almonds

Work butter, flour, almond extract, and sugar together until you have a smooth dough. It takes a while. In the beginning it will be crumbly, but as you work it, it will become smooth and pliable. Roll in long ropes about the size of a little finger, and cut into 2 inch pieces. Dip in egg white and then in the tinted almond-sugar mixture. Bake in a 400° oven for 10 minutes or until light brown.

FORMAR

For this cookie, a special pliable tart mold is used. As a rule, they can be bought in a Swedish gift shop.

1 egg   ½ teaspoon ammoniated
½ cup sugar   powder
1 cup butter   flour as needed

Beat the egg well and add sugar. Set aside.
Cream butter until light and fluffy. Add to egg mixture and add ammoniated powder. Work in flour until the dough can be handled; it should not be stiff.
Fill the bottom of each mold and place on a baking sheet. Bake at 400° for 12 to 15 minutes. Let stand a few minutes and then unmold.

KISSES

4 egg whites   1 cup sugar
1 tablespoon fresh lemon juice

Beat egg whites stiff and then beat in ⅔ cup sugar. Add lemon juice and fold in the rest of the sugar. Drop by heaping teaspoonfuls onto a greased baking sheet. Bake in a 200° oven for 1 hour. Then turn off the oven and let the cookies stand until the oven is cold.

UPPÅKRAKAKOR

10 tablespoons butter	1 egg
½ cup sugar	1½ cups flour
½ cup potato flour or cornstarch	

Cream the butter. Add sugar and cream again. Add unbeaten egg and work together. When well mixed, add both kinds of flour. Roll out on a baking board. (If too soft to roll, add more flour.) Prick all the dough with a fork. Cut with a fruit juice glass or a small round cutter. From the edge of each cookie, cut out one small place with a thimble. This gives the cookie a unique look. Bake in a 400° oven for 10 to 13 minutes or until very light brown. They should be very thin.

SMÖR STJÄRNOR

2 cups flour
½ pound butter
2 tablespoons heavy cream

Topping

beaten egg white
sugar
chopped pecans

Work the butter and flour together. Add cream and mix into a fairly stiff dough. Place in the refrigerator. When well chilled, roll out very thinly. Use plenty of flour on the board to keep the dough from sticking. Cut with a star cutter. Brush each cookie with beaten egg white and sprinkle with sugar and finely chopped pecans. Place on a greased cookie sheet. Bake in a 375° oven for about 10 minutes. Watch carefully and remove from the oven as soon as they begin to brown.

JUL-KAKOR

1 cup butter	2 teaspoons baking powder
1 cup sugar	2 tablespoons milk
2 eggs, beaten	1 teaspoon vanilla
2 cups flour mix together with	colored sugar

Cream the butter and sugar together. Add egg and cream again until light. Add flour, alternating with milk. (Flour is mixed with baking powder.) Add vanilla. Roll out on a baking board (after dividing the dough into three pieces). Roll each section separately. Cut out with cutters—bells, half moons, angels, oak leaves, et cetera. Brush the tops with just enough water to dampen, then sprinkle with colored sugar. Bake on greased cookie sheets in a 400° oven 10 to 15 minutes, according to the thickness of the cookie. This recipe makes about six dozen cookies.

CHRISTMAS *KRINGLOR*

1 cup sugar	2 eggs beaten
1 cup butter	2 teaspoons baking powder
½ cup milk	flour, as needed

Combine all of the above ingredients, using only enough flour to make the dough smooth and pliable. Push out through a cookie press, using a plain, round pattern. If you do not have a cookie press, roll out in long thin ropes. Cut into equal pieces and form into pretzel shapes. Place on greased baking sheets and bake in a 375° oven about 15 to 20 minutes or until golden brown.

STRUTAR

1 egg	⅓ cup flour
¼ cup sugar	nut meats, finely chopped

Beat the egg. Add sugar and beat again for 10 minutes. Fold in the flour. Place one heaping tablespoon of the mixture on

168

a greased baking sheet. Spread out with a spoon until it forms a large, round cookie. Sprinkle with nutmeats. Repeat the process. Bake in a 350° oven until light brown. Remove from the oven and loosen the cookies from the pan. With your fingers, shape each cookie into a cone, immediately. Work quickly for they soon harden and must be shaped while hot. If they begin to cool, replace the baking sheet in the oven and start again. Store in a tight jar or can.

FRUIT GOODIES

1 cup brown sugar	2 cups uncooked oatmeal
1 cup white sugar	½ teaspoon salt
½ teaspoon soda	2 cups flour
½ teaspoon baking powder	

Mix all the ingredients together thoroughly and spread one-quarter of the mixture on a greased 8x12 cake pan. Carefully spoon on a layer of filling and cover with another quarter of the mixture. The recipe fills two 8x12 pans, so repeat the above procedure. Bake in a 350° oven for 45 minutes.

FILLING

3 tablespoons flour	1½ cups hot water
1½ cups brown sugar	juice of ½ lemon
2 cups dried fruit	

Mix the flour and sugar well. Put the fruit through a food chopper and add to the mixture. Add water, stirring rapidly. Cook until thick. Let cool then add lemon juice. Use as directed above.

CORNFLAKE MACAROONS

2 egg whites	⅓ teaspoon vanilla
½ cup sugar	1 cup cornflakes
1 cup coconut	

Beat egg whites until they stand in stiff peaks. Fold in sugar, coconut, vanilla, and cornflakes. Drop onto greased baking sheets by the teaspoonful about 1½ inches apart. Bake in a 350° oven for 10 to 15 minutes.

PECAN BALLS

1 cup ground pecans	1 teaspoon vanilla
2 tablespoons sugar	1 cup all-purpose flour
½ cup butter	a pinch of salt
	confectioner's sugar

Mix the ground nuts, sugar, butter, vanilla, flour, and salt in a mixing bowl (use your hands) until smooth. Roll into balls the size of a small nut. Bake in a 375° oven on ungreased baking sheets for 20 minutes. When cool, roll in confectioner's sugar.

I usually bake my cookies right after December 13 which is the Swedish Lucia Day. It is a tradition; Mama did this and her Mama before her, so it seems only natural to follow in line. My older daughter has broken the tradition by having her cookies baked before the thirteenth, for she is always the Lucia bride herself. She dresses in white, wears a candle crown, and serves coffee to her family in bed, letting them taste all of the cookies. But I stick to the old rules.

The secret of a happy December is to get things done well in advance, leaving plenty of time to enjoy each new moment.

Wandering through the stores is a real experience. It is fun to mingle with the crowds as the old carols are played and people rush and push. Gifts have to be bought early, especially those which are to be sent out of town, so they are taken care of first. The guest room fills up with all sorts of packages and bundles. Then the wrapping starts, and that takes me far into the night. I like putting fancy bows on each package and writing something special on each name card. I wrap a part of my heart with each gift. I hope that when the person opens his package, he will know how much I loved to send it.

After all the out-of-town gifts have been mailed and all the others have been bought and wrapped, I take out my Christmas cards to sign and to write little notes. Sometimes I only have time to write a few lines such as, "I am thinking of you!" or "How I wish I could see you!" Even little greetings such as these add so much to friendship. There is a feeling of satisfaction when that last bundle of cards goes into the post office, and already my basket for incoming cards is beginning to fill. I always get the greatest thrill over the first card to arrive. Every Christmas season I feel the same way—the wonder of it! I hold it in my hand and read its message over and over, and I think of the dear person who sent it.

When my husband comes home, I meet him with the same words: "Dear, do you know what happened today?"

He looks at my beaming face and says calmly, "I wouldn't be surprised if the first Christmas card had arrived."

"How did you know?" I exclaim.

"You always look like this. It is there every year, that look in your eyes, as if something wonderful had happened."

Perhaps it is foolish to be so excited over just a card, but it is part of me, part of my happiness, seeing things come to pass and loving them so much.

Soon I remind Bob that it is time to pick out the Christmas tree and to get all the lights wired on the bushes. That is his job, but I like to see them go on before we get a real cold spell with snow covering the evergreens. So we put them up long before we light them, just to have everything ready. Picking out the Christmas tree is something we do together, and it takes a long time because we have different ideas of how a tree should look. I like a real tight tree with the branches close together. Bob thinks there should be spaces between the branches, knowing very well how filled in it will be when all the decorations are on it. But I usually win, and we take the tree home and leave it in a pail of water in the back yard. Of course, the water often freezes and the tree stands there in a cake of ice. But at least it will be there when we are ready for it, and that worry is over.

I also have other lists I have made years ago, and I take them out each Christmas season. These are a "must" every year in the middle of December.

To be baked:
Limpabread (ryebread, page 10)
Coffee bread (page 35)
Cupcakes (use the Tårta recipe, page 36, and put in cupcake tins)
Mjuk Pepparkaka

This list, in addition to the cookie list, takes care of my baking. The secret of the Mjuk Pepparkaka is that the longer you keep it, the better it tastes.

MJUK PEPPARKAKA

½ cup butter
2 cups light brown sugar
2 eggs
1 teaspoon baking soda dissolved in little warm water

½ teaspoon ginger
½ teaspoon cinnamon
½ teaspoon cloves
2 cups sifted cake flour
1 cup milk

Cream butter and add the sugar, mixing well with electric beater. In another bowl beat eggs until very light and add to first mixture. Add baking soda and spices. Fold in flour, alternating with the milk, and mix well.

Bake in 350° oven in a large tube pan which has been well greased with plenty of butter and dusted with breadcrumbs. The baking time is 35 minutes. Let cake cool before removing from pan.

My list also includes washing the curtains and the windows. There is something extra special about clean curtains for Christmas and the work is well worth the effort. To me, the house has a new look when all the windows are shiny and festive.

Next on my list is planning the Smörgåsbord menu and buying candles. Here in America I don't follow a completely Swedish smörgåsbord pattern. There are so many things that my children and grandchildren don't like. I have broadened my menu to include many American foods so that the feast of this blessed evening will make everybody happy. The menu varies from year to year, but there are many old stand-bys that I would never omit. That would change old traditions, which I never could do.

CHRISTMAS EVE SMÖRGÅSBORD

Baked ham   Roast turkey   Swedish sausage   Christmas-*sylta*
Meatballs   Thuringer   Liverwurst
Cooked shrimp in cocktail sauce
Cocktail frankfurts
Chicken salad
Potato salad   Molded fruit salad   Tossed salad
Green bean casserole   Macaroni and cheese   Baked beans
Sardines   Anchovy spears   Pickled herring
Deviled eggs   *Bondost*   Blue cheese
Pickled beets   Swedish cucumbers
Dill pickles
Lingonberries
Swedish rye bread   Rolls   Hardtack
Fruit Soup with whipped cream
Christmas cookies
Cider   Coffee

Each dish has to be decorated with curly parsley, spiced crabapples, or fruits. And, of course, many live candles and greens make this the loveliest table setting of the whole year.

I like to get the house completely cleaned a week before Christmas Eve. This, of course, does not eliminate the daily dusting and vacuuming. After that, Bob will carry up the big boxes of decorations from the cellar, and little by little, I take out those dear ornaments, some of which have been with Bob and me since our first Christmas together. We had only a few decorations then, but in forty years we have accumulated so many that the whole house is transformed into a real Christmas land. I usually take one room at a time, removing the knickknacks and everyday ornaments, packing them away, and bringing

174

out the Swedish holiday decorations with their gay colors and meaningful drawings. Then out come the candles and lights. There are candles everywhere—in candelabras, in wooden candle sticks, in iron holders. Then, of course, there are the beautiful big artificial candles that stand on our front steps, and lights in each of our windows. Outside the big spruce in the back yard and the evergreens in the front yard are lit up, and the lantern by the driveway has a red light that matches the big red bow on the door wreath. Everything is aglow, reflecting the joy and happiness and peace in our household.

I try to have everything decorated a few days before December 24. Then comes the last-minute cooking and the baking of the rye bread and the coffee bread.

We keep lots of extra grain on hand so that the birds can share in Christmas. And even Gretchen wears a big red bow on her collar.

"It is Christmas, Gretchen," I tell her, "and for a few days you will be a Christmas symbol, too, and greet all our guests."

At last all is ready. Only then can I permit myself the luxury of relaxing and thinking back to Christmases of long ago when we were children and Papa and Mama were our whole world. It is good to remember the peace there was and the stillness and calm as Christmas Eve approached. Mama was busy preparing little remembrances for otherwise forgotten people in the community —a box of cookies here, a coffee ring there, a little plant to someone in a hospital ward—little gifts, over and above her budget, but gifts from our household to the Christ child. There was a pair of hand-knitted mittens for the retarded boy in a poor family. For the recently orphaned little girl living with unwilling relatives, Mama had a gay coloring book and some cookies from her Christmas baking. A loaf of rye bread went to our next-door neighbors. Yes, Mama sent us children all over the village with Christmas cheer. But there was one particular Christmas I'll never forget when Mama sent me on a strange mission.

In a shack at the edge of the village, there lived an ugly old recluse. He was a strange man with a badly disfigured face, and he seemed to hate children. There were all kinds of rumors about him. Some people said he was rich and hoarded his money, having sacks of it hidden away. But it was just gossip; no one knew for sure. Anyway, everyone was afraid of him and we children tried to avoid walking near his place. But this Christmas Eve Mama had been thinking about him.

"It is Christmas for him, too," she said, "and we must make a little treat for him. I want you to go and knock on his door to give him this bundle and wish him a Merry Christmas."

"But I am afraid of him, Mama," I said.

"You need never be afraid when you go in the name of love, carrying good tidings on a Christmas Eve," said Mama with a smile.

I took the bundle, surprised that it felt warm. I looked questioningly at Mama.

"It is a chicken I cooked for him," Mama informed me, "and some little things to go with it. Be careful not to tip it."

I started off through the snow, thinking how brave I was, visiting this man who always chased children away.

But inside, I trembled a little. Well, I thought, if he is mean, I can always leave the bundle and run.

It certainly did not look like Christmas around his shack, but I knocked at the door and waited, clasping my bundle close to me.

Then I heard dragging feet coming toward the door, and it was opened just a crack.

"What do you want?" the old man barked.

"Mama sent me to bring you some Christmas cheer. This is a gift for you."

Slowly the door opened wide. "Come in," he said.

I stepped inside, keeping close to the door, looking around the room. It was the messiest room I had ever seen, and it was cold and dark.

"I am the pastor's little girl," I said. "I want to wish you a Merry Christmas."

"What have you got in the bundle?"

"A chicken—and things."

He took the bundle and unwrapped it; then his eyes grew big and round. "Is it all for me?"

"Yes." I cleared my voice. "It is to remind you of the Christ child."

He wiped his nose and blew it hard. It was hard to tell for sure, but I thought I saw a tear rolling down that ugly face.

"Sit down," he said kindly.

I sat down on the chair by the table.

"Say thank you to your Mama and I—will—I will thank the Christ child myself."

The chicken smelled so good in that tiny kitchen littered with papers and cans that I became a little bolder.

"May I straighten up your place a little to make it look more like Christmas?" I asked him, because suddenly I wasn't afraid of him any more. I just felt sorry that he was so alone.

He nodded and I picked up what I could and wiped the table and tried to fix the food Mama had sent so it looked nice. He did not look mean any more; he looked almost nice. Then a thought came into my mind.

"Would you like to come home with me to have Christmas with us?" I asked.

He shook his head.

"No, I'd like to stay here in my world, but this is the first time anyone ever gave me anything. It will be a good Christmas Eve."

I began to get ready to leave, still feeling sorry he was alone.

He held me back. "Stay a minute," he said. "I'd like to share a Christmas story with you."

I sat down on a chair, and he sat down beside me.

"Can I read the Christmas story for you?" I asked, picking up his dusty old Bible.

"No, thank you, little girl. I'll tell you a Christmas story now and later tonight I'll read the story of the first Christmas myself."

His eyes were shining now and his scarred face was almost handsome.

"Once I had a little girl like you," he said slowly, looking out the window off into the distance. "I had a nice home and a wife, too. Then one Christmas Eve my little girl wanted to light the candles on our Christmas tree. I never should have let her, but she pleaded so that I gave in. She dropped the match and the tree went up in flames; and so did our home. My wife and little girl were so badly burned that they did not live to see another year. As you can see, I myself was burned. I wanted to die, too, but I lived. So I moved away from there. I bought this old place and I became a recluse . . . working just enough to buy food. I hated life and everybody . . . and God . . . and most of all, Christmas. Many years have gone by, but no one ever befriended me until tonight. You came, almost like my little Dagmar and it was Christmas Eve . . ."

He stopped suddenly, blowing his nose again. I went over and put my arms around him.

"This hug is from your little girl up in Heaven," I told him.

What a strange Christmas Eve that was as I sat at our table with our happy family. I felt that I had so much. That next week Papa and Mama went to see the old man, but by the time the new year had come, he had left this earth. He was a different man those last days because Christmas had touched his heart with love. A silver key could not have opened this man's heart, but the pure gold of love did, and all because Mama gave her gifts to the Christ child.

Let us not forget to remember those who need love at this time of the year, for that is the only true way of celebrating Christmas.

Now, let us take a look at the Christmas Eve food. So many things on this smörgåsbord are simply prepared foods with which every housewife is familiar. The Swedish sausage can be bought in a Swedish delicatessen or a Scandinavian food store; so can the *bondost* (cheese) and the pickled herring. But the following are, perhaps, unfamiliar recipes:

CHRISTMAS-*SYLTA*

1 pound side pork	3 whole cloves
1 pound veal shank	1 small onion
2¼ cups water	1 tablespoon vinegar
1 tablespoon salt	white pepper to taste
5 whole allspice	1 teaspoon gelatine (dissolved in a little water)
6 white pepper corns	
2 bay leaves	

Bring the meat to boiling in the 2¼ cups water. Skim off the top and add the seasonings and onion. Simmer 1½ hours or until tender. Remove from the stove and cut into tiny cubes. Return the bones to the stock and cook 30 minutes. Strain the stock, return to kettle, add meat and cook 15 minutes. Add white pepper to taste, vinegar, and gelatine.

Pour into a mold that has been rinsed in cold water and dried. Chill. Unmold in time for serving. Decorate with slices of pickled beets.

GREEN BEAN CASSEROLE

Cook frozen French-style green beans as directed. Season with salt and pepper and put into a buttered casserole. Pour one can of cream of mushroom soup over the beans and top with large slices of frozen onions. Sprinkle on bread crumbs and dot with butter.

Bake in 300° oven for 15 minutes.

There may be other specialties you'd like to put on your Christmas Eve table, things your family likes, so you add your own creations, too.

After Christmas Day come the cooky parties at our house. The week between Christmas and the New Year, when the wonder of Christmas Eve with its delicious smörgåsbord and the family opening their gifts together is over, when Christmas Day with its warmth and feasting has come to a close, when the candles glow and the house smells of pine boughs and hemlock and the delicate flavor of food and all that work has paid in dividends of love and joy, it is then that the week begins, the last week of the year. The house bears on its door an unwritten invitation that says, "Drop in to see us!" It is then that the cookies are set out on a table which stands ready at all times for company. I think I love this week more than any other week in the year, and those cookies are so lovely to look at and taste so good. I forget at times that I am in America and in the old-country tradition I pass the tray saying, "Please do take another one. . . . Just one more. . . . You haven't tasted the *uppåkrakakor* yet; they really are good. . . ." That is how it was in the old times. Housewives were so anxious for their guests to taste every kind of cooky on the table, and the urging went on until a new set of faces were seated around the never-ending coffee table.

It is Christmas all over the world. Lights shine and music plays and company comes and goes throughout this blessed season. What a way to usher out a month, to see it slip away. And with December goes the year. The holy days are over, and soon life begins again in its normal way. And although there are parties and celebrations, we might take a moment to stop to think about the year that has gone forever.

The gift of years! What a challenge they are and how much God has entrusted to us. They gave us so much, but what did we give to them? What do we leave behind us that is of strength and value? Perhaps they were not a gift at all, but just a loan from God. I hope that we have done our best. And as we begin a brand-new year, may we tread prayerfully with careful feet so that the heart of the home can beat triumphantly.

To start a new year is to be given a new chance to build even stronger ties and deeper understanding within the family, and nothing in the world can destroy a family like that. It will go from happiness to happiness, leaving a solid foundation for the next generation to build on.

GOLD NUGGET:

The greatest gift at Christmas time is to let the Christ give Himself to us.

As Father Time lets his shadow fall over the year which has just closed and my book which is now finished, there is a feeling of completeness in my soul. Together we have walked softly through the months and now, as the year is full of days, I pray that our hearts have been touched by the tenderness of God's love.

As we look back, we have had so much and the heart of the home beats in a happy rhythm to the melody of joy. Our cup is full and runneth over.

I put my pen down, knowing that there is so much goodness everywhere and that the darkness can never snuff out the flame which was lit by God's love to our world.

℘ INDEX

A

Angel-food delight, 62–63
Apple(s)
   -*kaka,* 23–24
   pie, 103
   yams and marshmallows
      with, 157
Apricot bars, 159–160
   filling for, 160
April menus, 49–52
August menus, 101–108

B

Bacon
   and cheddar cheese sand-
      wiches, 140–141
   tiny bit broils, 153
Banana cake supreme, 123
   vanilla glaze for, 124

Beans
   green, 157
      casserole, 180
      French, 50
   wax, French style, 138
Beets, Harvard, 139
Birthdays, 25–29
   peppar-kakor, 37–38
   spritz cookies, 37
   Swedish *kaka,* 35–36
      toppings, 36
   tårta, 36
Blood stains, removing, 78
Blue cheese bread, 139
Blueberry quicky muffins, 93
Bread
   oatmeal, 123
   shredded-wheat, 50–51
   Swedish rye, 9–10
   Vienna blue cheese, 139
Bridal showers, 43–49
   entertainment, 48–49
Brown sugar, grating, 38

Buns
cinnamon, 103–104
schnecken, 61–62
filling, 62
Butter balls, 139
Butterscotch rolls, 158

C

Cake(s)
angel-food delight, 62–63
apple-*kaka,* 23–24
banana supreme, 123
vanilla glaze for, 124
birthday *kaka,* 35–36
topping, 36
chocolate, 141
frosting, 141–142
coffee, 46–47
four o'clock skorpor, 114
cupcakes, 107–108
mjuk peppar-kaka, 173
strawberry shortcake, 78
tårta, 36
Carrots deluxe, 61
Casseroles
green bean, 180
onion, 157
salmon, 60–61
Cheddar cheese
and bacon sandwiches, 140–141
tiny bit broils, 153
Cherries, removing pits from, 12

Chicken
fried, 102
salad, 77
Chives, potato salad with, 102–103
Chocolate
cake, 141
frosting, 141–142
wafers, 47–48
Christmas; 161–181
kringlor, 168
menus, 165–169, 172, 174, 180
sylta, 180
Cinnamon buns, 103–104
Coffee cake, 46–47
four o'clock skorpor, 114
Cookies
chocolate wafers, 47–48
Christmas *kringlor,* 168
cornflake macaroons, 169–170
drommar, 165
finska brod, 165–166
formar, 166
fruit goodies, 169
jul-kakor, 168
kisses, 47, 166–167
oatmeal, 104
pecan balls, 170
peppar-kakor, 37–38
smor stjärnor, 167
spritz, 37
strutar, 168–169
uppakra kakor, 167
Corn pudding, 77

J

January menus, 9–12
Jelly, rose-hip, 83
Jul-kakor, 168
July menus, 83–84, 92–94
June menus, 76–78

K

Kaka
    apple-, 23–24
    birthday, 35–36
    socker-, 114–115
Kakor
    jul-, 168
    peppar-, 37–38
    uppakra, 167
Kåldormar, 121–122
Kisses, 47, 166–167
Klippkrans, 46–47
Kringlor, Christmas, 168

L

Lamb, roast leg of, 137–138
    gravy for, 138
Lent, 30
Lettuce salad, 158
Linen, fruit stains on, 64

M

Macaroons, cornflake, 169–170
March menus, 33–38

Marshmallows with yams and apples, 157
May menus, 60–63
Meatballs, 50
Menus
    January, 9–12
    February, 22–24
    March, 33–38
    April, 49–52
    May, 60–63
    June, 76–78
    July, 83–84, 92–94
    August, 101–108
    September, 114–115, 121–124
    October, 136–141
    November, 152–153, 154–160
    December, 165–169, 172, 174, 180
Mjuk peppar-kaka, 173
Muffins, quicky blueberry, 93

N

November menus, 152–153, 154–160
Nypon-Soppa, 83–84

O

Oatmeal
    bread, 123
    cookies, 104
October menus, 136–141
Omelet, fluffy, 152–153
Onion casserole, 157

P

Pancakes, 34
Parsley, keeping fresh, 24
Passover, 32
Pea soup, 33–34
Peach and cottage cheese salad, 141
Pear-and-cream-cheese salad, 139
Peas, fresh garden, 93
Pecan
    balls, 170
    tarts, 48
Peppar-kakor, 37–38
Picnics, 101–104
Pies
    apple, 103
    pineapple cream, 140
    strawberry-rhubarb, 93–94
Pineapple cream pie, 140
Plättar, 34
Plätt-panna, 33, 34
Popovers, 78
Potato(es)
    de luxe creamed, 92–93
    mashed, 156
    patties, 22–23
    roasted, 138
    salad with chives, 102–103
Pudding, corn, 77

Q

Quick rusks, 84
Quicky blueberry muffins, 93

R

Rhubarb-strawberry pie, 93–94
Rolls, butterscotch, 158
Rose(s)
    beads, 81–82
    -hip jelly, 83
    -hip soup, 83–84
    jar, 82
Rot-mos, 10–11
Rusks, 84
Russian dressing, 158
Rye bread, 9–10

S

Salad
    chicken, 77
    frozen, 106–107
    lettuce, 158
    peach and cottage cheese, 141
    pear-and-cream-cheese, 139
    potato with chives, 102–103
    spinach, 152
    tossed, 61
Salmon casserole, 60–61
Sandwiches, 140–141
    picnic, 104
Sauces
    angel-food delight, 63
    cream, 157
    vanilla, 24